GREAT DISASTERS

OF THE WORLD

GREAT DISASTERS
OF THE WORLD

By Beryl Frank

GALAHAD BOOKS · NEW YORK CITY

Thanks to all of the following people who helped in the preparation of this book on disasters and who insured the fact that the author would not become the final disaster in the book:

To Vince Mele and Elma Masut of Wide World Photos, Inc.

To all patient librarians, wherever they may be

To Carol Wynne who helped immeasureably

To Editor Ruth Cogley

And of course, and always, to Lou.

Table of Contents

Introduction

WHAT IS A DISASTER?

Any happening that causes great harm or damage; serious or sudden misfortune; calamity.

In the context of this book, a tragedy must not be confused with a disaster. A tragedy in the literal sense refers to unhappy endings brought about by fate (as in the Greek tragic plays), by moral weakness or social pressures. The assassinations of President Abraham Lincoln or Martin Luther King were tragedies. They may have caused disasterous events afterwards, but in themselves, they were not disasters. On the other hand, the Beverly Hills Fire in Kentucky which killed hundreds of people and the Jonestown Massacre which did the same were disasters.

The number of people listed as dead in a disaster often cause the researcher problems. Early reports are sometimes contradicted by later facts as to the number of dead. In this book, the figures used are those most often listed in major sources.

The use of the words "greatest" and "worst" have not often been included in this book. This author has no gauge as to what was the "worst" flood in history (unless Noah's flood is included) or what was the "greatest" explosion of all time. Every disaster could be described in superlatives. Loss of life and loss of property have both increased in modern times with increased population and increased urbanization. But this in no way diminishes the disaster at Pompeii in A.D. 79. In short, each disaster included here is a story of death and destruction in itself. There is no greatest. There is no worst.

War and war-related disasters are not included here. Since these are evidences of man's inhumanity to man, they do not belong in a book which deals with unavoidable calamities and acts of nature.

Finally, although the time span covered in this book ranges from A.D. 79 to the 1980s, no book could possibly include every disaster which has occured to mankind. Eruptions of nature have repeated themselves over and over again as have man-made accidents. What has also repeated itself has been man's heroism in the face of all kinds of disasters. Hopefully, man can learn from what this book shows of the past.

EARLY DISASTERS

The Black Cloud of Death from Vesuvius

The Black Death of Europe

The Great Fire of London

THE BLACK CLOUD OF DEATH FROM VESUVIUS

Mount Vesuvius, standing 4000 feet high, still towers over the modern city of Naples, Italy. Two thousand years ago, this volcano was described as ''a cone-shaped mountain with a flat top, on which was a circular valley filled with vines and grass and surrounded by high precipices.'' The description could very well hold true today.

After Greek civilization gave way to the golden years of Rome, Roman colonists chose to settle in the communities surrounding Vesuvius. The area was good for cultivation on all sides of the volcano, and such cities as Herculaneum and Pompeii flourished. Nobody feared Vesuvius at that time, since they believed the volcano was dead. Thus, luxurious villas overlooking the Bay of Naples were built by wealthy Romans without a thought to a volcanic eruption. None could conceive that the mighty Vesuvius would ever belch forth debris and gasses which would bury thousands of people alive where they stood.

In A.D. 63, 16 years before Vesuvius raged, Pompeii lay victim to a great earthquake—one which nearly destroyed the city. The restoration work was not quite finished when Vesuvius expelled its poisonous gas and volcanic matter.

This view of Mt. Vesuvius shows the eruption as it might have looked to the residents of Pompeii.

Although there was no warning of the violent eruption which began on August 24, A.D. 79, there was still enough time before destruction for some of the citizens to flee. Those who chose to disregard the first eruption, however, met their doom. For eight days, the ''dead'' volcano continued to spew out rock, gasses and smoke—with such force at times that the clouds which formed reached thousands of feet into the air.

A seventeen-year-old Roman, whom historians named Pliny the Younger, was staying with relatives in Misenum (19 miles from Pompeii) when Vesuvius wrought its destruction. In his eye-witness account of the eruptions, he compared what he saw to ''a pine tree, for it shot to a great height like a trunk and extended itself at the top into a kind of branch . . .'' He also reported that the cloud which covered the sun was sometimes bright and sometimes dark and spotted. Indeed, it must have been an awesome sight to see.

The heat and pressure that rose from deep within the bowels of the earth erupted with such force that volcanic matter which reached the upper atmosphere expanded and, thus, released great clouds of poisonous gas.

With the first eruption on August 24, the streets of Pompeii were covered with six feet of volcanic ash. Millions of tons of ash were still to fall, in addition to the noxious steam and vapor that spread death as it moved earthward.

Last of all the horror, yet definitely not least, was a flood of water down the mountainside. It its course, the water mixed with mud to form a heavy volcanic paste. It was this paste that was the preservative agent which allowed excavators to reconstruct the end of such cities as Pompeii and Herculaneum many centuries later.

Black smoke and ash rained down on the city of Pompeii, burying it and all who were there in volcanic paste.

What were the people in Pompeii doing when Vesuvius erupted? The bodies of gladiators were found in a sports arena, preserved as they died in volcanic paste. Loaves of bread were uncovered in the ovens where they had been baking. Sealed jugs of olives, fruit and wine were found with their contents unharmed.

When the Temple of Isis was uncovered, a priest was found seated at his meal. Two Roman soldiers were found still locked in the stocks where they had been punished at the time of the eruption. One skeleton was uncovered near the prison with a handful of silver coins still clutched by the bones of its hand.

In private homes, people were found imprisoned in the volcanic paste in the positions they had been standing in. One woman was found with her hands raised above her head to ward off the caving roof. Jewelry which she had dropped was scattered on the floor nearby.

The estimated death toll from this catastrophe is 16,000 people. The eruption from Vesuvius in A.D. 79 was not to be the last; however, it was one of the most serious. Through the years, the city of Pompeii has stood as a memorial to those who lost their lives during Vesuvius' reigning eight days of terror.

After the devastating eruption of A.D. 79, Mt. Vesuvius returned to its previously quiet state. A small column of smoke was all that attested to the fact that the volcano was sleeping and might someday erupt again.

Millions Die

The statistics of the Black Death—or bubonic plague—are so great that they are almost unbelievable. Five hundred bodies of the afflicted dead were thrown daily into mass graves on the outskirts of Paris. England buried its dead. Italy lost half of its population to the dreaded scourge. In short, one-third of the population of Europe died of the plague.

What was the Black Death? The disease was a three-day killer which originated in the far east. It reached the Crimea by approximately 1347. A ship from the Crimean port of Kaffa returned to Genoa at about that time. Along with spices from the east, the ship carried rats—big, black-eared rats—who left the ship for the city in search of food. There must have been hundreds or even thousands of these rats entering Genoa—and they were not only infected with the disease themselves, but they also had fleas. Hence, the fleas fed on the rats and then later attached themselves to humans. It was by means of these flea bites that the Black Death was spread among the populace.

The Black Death

The first symptoms of the disease were headaches and high fevers. These were followed by shivering and dizziness. Next came hard, black boils which showed themselves under the armpits and in the groin area. The color black came from blood clots under the skin; it was from these clots that the common name of Black Death was used instead of the more scientific bubonic plague. The final stage of the illness was the extreme vomiting of blood. Death followed shortly after this.

The rapidity with which the Black Death spread is shocking. In a period of four short years, people in Europe were dying by the millions. It was because there were so many corpses that the dead could not be buried in individual graves.

"Dead men," as they were called, walked the streets of major European cities pushing huge carts to collect the victims of the disease. Family members of the afflicted put the dead in the streets where the "dead men" collected them for mass burial. Sometimes, live people were mistakenly collected as well.

Many of the wealthier people were able to leave the cities for country estates—but even this did not protect them from the disease. The fleas were no respecters of wealth or country. From Switzerland to Germany, from France to England and even as far away as Russia and North Africa, the disease ran rampant.

Remedies to cure the Black Death were unsuccessful but numerous. Doctors hesitated to declare the disease incurable and so resorted to many different approaches. One of the most common remedies was the use of leeches. Many plague victims succumbed to repeated leechings before they reached the final stages of the disease and died.

To the already superstitious people of the 14th Century, the plague was a reason to wear charms and amulets to ward off the disease. Needless to say, these charms were of no use. People were accused of witchcraft by the score and many died by fire. And still the doctors tried to find remedies.

Sometimes doctors prescribed rubbing lard or butter into open wounds. This was one of the more humane treatments. However, like other and more violent cures, this failed.

One of the more promising treatments for the disease was to surgically open the boils and then cauterize the open wound with a red-hot poker. If the patient survived the pain of this treatment, which was without benefit of any anesthetic, there was a slight chance of a cure. Once cured, the victim was then immune and could safely help to care for others who were ill.

For those five years in the 14th Century, the Black Death was at its peak, killing people by the hundreds of thousands. However, people continued to die of the plague for another 300 years. No one knows why the plague ceased to be a mass murderer by the middle of the 17th Century. But, by the year 1666—the date of the London Fire—the Black Death seemed to disappear. Were the people of Europe at last cleaning up their cities? Since the plague germ was spread by unsanitary living conditions, this is perhaps an answer. No one can say for sure.

Today, modern science and medicine have almost eradicated the Black Death. Scientists discovered and isolated the plague germ at the end of the 19th Century. Early in the 20th Century, it was proven that the disease was carried by flea-ridden rats. These discoveries, however, came much too late for the world of 1347. The Black Death had already wiped out one-third of the European population.

The citizens of London threw their furnishings and personal belongings into the narrow streets in an effort to save what they could.

A 20th-Century writer described London as "a city whose beauties never end." While this may be true today, it was definitely not so in the days before the Great Fire of London in 1666.

London, 1666

At that time, London was a crowded city of narrow streets and tall buildings. The upper stories of the houses were constructed so that they hung out over the narrow streets below. When houses of this fashion were built on both sides of the street, there was almost no light in the street at all. Open gutters lined the sidewalks, and the citizen who went out for a daily stroll did so at the risk of having garbage fall on his head from the windows above.

The streets of London were fetid due to the garbage which lay in them. The filth and dirt had undoubtedly contributed to the spread of the bubonic plague in the preceding year. This situation was certainly inviting to the flames which were soon to come.

Where the Great Fire actually began is open to conjecture. The most commonly accepted version states that the fire started in the shop of Thomas Farynor. Farynor was the King's baker and the shop was located on Pudding Lane. Sparks quickly spread from Farynor's shop to the hay and fodder stored in an open yard of a nearby inn.

From there, the fire traveled to nearby warehouses and wharves, where such flammables as tallow, oil, hay and coal were licked to life by the crackling flames. In a very short time, the city of London was burning like a giant candle.

Two noted diarists of the time, Samuel Pepys and John Evelyn, wrote descriptions of what they saw. One or both of these men made haste to warn the court of King Charles II at Whitehall. The King ordered that houses should be torn down at once, thereby forming firebreaks to halt the spreading flames.

At first, the Lord Mayor of London refused to order this destruction. Finally, he complied with the King's command and buildings were razed by fire fighters. However, this did little to stop the appetite of the fire. In fact, the new man-made ruins added more fuel to the flames.

Some Londoners rushed to the Thames river in an attempt to escape from the roaring blaze which swept through the city.

The fire which raged in the city of London began on September 2, 1666. This engraving shows the city as seen from Ludgate.

The Burning of St. Paul's

On September 3, the fire made its way to St. Paul's Cathedral. At the time, St. Paul's was undergoing repairs and there was wooden scaffolding set up on all sides. This scaffolding caught fire and soon the entire building was in flames. The lead roof melted, crashing to the floor below and destroying everything that was stored there. Along with the rest of London, St. Paul's had to be rebuilt after the Great Fire. (The architect Christopher Wren was to design many of the new buildings in London, including St. Paul's Cathedral.)

London was to burn for five long days before the fire was halted. Miraculously, only a few people—some records say only six—died as a result of the fire. Many Londoners had left the city by boat on the Thames River and so escaped from the blaze; others were able to keep ahead of the flames and so save their own lives—if not their possessions.

While the Great Fire did not take many lives, the toll in property destruction was huge. Three-hundred and seventy-three acres inside the city walls were laid waste in ashes. Sixty-three acres outside were also burned to the ground. Eighty-seven churches and over 13,000 houses were all alight before the Great Fire burned itself out.

Despite the effects of the Great Fire of London, the people were not dismayed. Within days of the final sparks, plans were underway to rebuild the city. London was to come forth from the ashes of this disaster as a cleaner and more beautiful place than the city had ever been before.

St. Paul's Cathedral was only one of the many buildings which burned in the Great Fire of London. Rescue attempts were made by using ladders to help free those trapped in nearby buildings.

1800s

When the Irish peasants began to dig their potatoes in the year 1845, what they dug up from the ground was blackened, blighted and inedible. Since the potato was the only staple food crop for the Irish poor, the potato blight was devastating.

The Irish peasants were considered to be among the world's most downtrodden, and the poverty in Ireland prior to 1845 was most extreme. Some of the English gentry noted this situation, but did nothing much except wring their hands at existing conditions.

In 1843, England appointed the Devon Commission to study the situation in Ireland. A report submitted that year stated:

"... In many districts, their (the Irish) only food is the potato, their only beverage water ... their cabins are seldom a protection against the weather ... a bed or a blanket is a rare luxury ... and nearly in all, their pig and manure heap constitute their only property."

With the advent of the potato blight in 1845, even these conditions worsened. But the English continued to pay no heed.

Ireland was a country of wealthy landlords with destitute peasants occupying a patch of land on their estates. Many of these landlords lived in England as absentee landlords—and these were the most hated by the Irish poor.

Most of the landlords, whether abroad or in residence, charged heavy rents to the people who worked their land. These rents included corn, wheat and cattle—all of which were raised for export to England. The common man in Ireland saw only the potato for his own use. Even this was the poorest type of potato—a gray tuber which was only used as pig feed in other parts of the world.

The landlords' purses grew fat with the money they received in rents, but not so for the Irishmen who had performed the labor.

The English were not overly concerned with Ireland's plight. What half-hearted efforts they made did little to ease the problem. They continued to import Ireland's produce while the Irish peasants continued to starve to death.

Hatred of the landlords was understandable. In County Mayo, for example, the Earl of Lucan evicted more than 40,000 peasants from their homes. At the slightest whim, they threw people off of their land. Men, women and children were thrust out, usually in winter, when the icy temperatures finished off what starvation had started. The Earl of Lucan was one of the most hated landlords, yet his action was applauded by the English press.

New World—New Hope

Those Irish who could manage to emigrate from the Emerald Isle did so. Approximately 1,000,000 men, women and children scraped up the money for passage and did endure the difficult two-month sea voyage to America. Most settled in the United States and Canada—and those who made it were indeed the lucky ones.

Those who had to remain in Ireland saw death all around them. People who were still in their hovels were found dead in their beds. Those who had been evicted from their homes died in the roadways as they fell. In addition to famine, disease broke out. Cholera, dysentery and typhus all took their toll on the starving Irishmen.

The cemetaries could not hold all of the dead, and gravediggers (weakened by hunger and disease) did not have the strength to dig deep into the earth. As a result, coffins which were placed shallowly in the ground were dug up by starving dogs who then consumed parts of the dead. Ireland was indeed a nightmare of disease and starvation.

The potato crop in Ireland failed for six consecutive years. The loss of this food staple caused the death of many people and the departure of others from the country of their birth. The population of Ireland was reduced by about one-fourth.

Feelings against the oppression of the English were to remain high in Ireland for generations, until rebellion and, finally, freedom came. Despite this freedom, the years of the "Great Famine" are years which will never be forgotten.

The Great Chicago Fire raged from Sunday evening until early Tuesday morning. As this old print shows, the blaze swept through the city of over 300,000 people, leaving 90,000 homeless and causing millions of dollars worth of property damage.

Conflicting Theories On Origin

Catherine O'Leary and her cow have achieved undying fame due to the Chicago Fire of October 8, 1871. There are many theories surrounding the mysterious start of the blaze, the most popular being that Mrs. O'Leary's cow kicked over a kerosene lamp in the barn and started the conflagration. The less celebrated postulations, though, suggest that some boys (smoking secretly in a haymow) or even a rat (gnawing on a matchhead) started the flames.

Whichever of these ideas you prefer, the fact remains that the fire started in a barn on De Koven Street in a crowded residential section of Chicago.

Chicago, 1871

What was the city of Chicago like at this time? A population of over 300,000 inhabitants had made Chicago a thriving metropolis by the year 1871. The city's growth had indeed mushroomed during the brief 40 year span from approximately 200 people in 1830.

Trainloads of immigrants were constantly arriving from the East. Businesses boomed and wooden housing was quickly thrown together to accommodate the thousands of people who kept pouring into the city. Even the sidewalks were made of wood. Thus, the city of Chicago was highly flammable!

Drought Turns City Into Tinderbox

But there is more to the Chicago Fire than a city ripe for burning. The summer of 1871 had been a time of extreme drought. Although there was some relief in early July, no rain had fallen since then. Reports of forest fires in nearby Wisconsin and Minnesota, also affected by the drought, showed the entire area to be ready kindling.

On Saturday night, October 7, a general alarm fire burned over 16 acres before Chicago fire fighters could control it. In addition to the loss of two pieces of fire-fighting equipment, the men who had fought the blaze were tired to the point of exhaustion.

At approximately 8:45 p.m., the De Koven Street fire broke out and spread rapidly from one tinderbox to another. The few buckets of water thrown on the flames by the home owners did nothing to halt the advance of the blaze.

This actual photograph of the debris shows a man trying to cool off a safe at what remained of the Fifth National Bank on Washington Street.

The first alarm sounded was from an alarm box 3½ blocks from De Koven Street. The man who ran those blocks found the alarm box locked, as this was customary to prevent the turning in of false alarms.

Little remained of the downtown area of Chicago after the Great Fire. The city faced massive reconstruction from the ashes.

An artist's rendering shows refugees fleeing over the Randolph Street bridge to safety on the west side. Although there were only 250-300 people killed in the fire, the number of inhabitants left homeless was staggering.

Locating the key to the alarm box took still more time. When the box was finally opened and the alarm pulled, nothing happened. The connections in the box did not work. This delay allowed the fire to gain a firmer hold in the wooden residential district.

Still another human error was to aid the fire's appetite. A lookout posted high in the tower of the courthouse misjudged where he saw the flames. As a result, fire equipment was sent more than a mile away from the actual blaze. Had this error been quickly noted and equipment sent to the right place, it is possible that the city of Chicago might not have burned.

Winds of 30 miles an hour helped to fan the flames and spread the fire, as did the strong updrafts from the fire itself. Flying brands started structures burning in all directions. The local gasworks caught fire and broken gas receivers added fuel to the blaze. The business district was alight, and buildings which claimed to be fireproof burned to the ground.

The fire raged out of control for many hours. It was not until Monday evening on October 9 that relief finally came to the aid of the 185 exhausted firemen. Rain came to Chicago—enough rain to finally put out the fires of the preceding 24 hours.

EPILOGUE

Seventeen-thousand buildings were destroyed. Losses were estimated to be $200 million. Only 250 to 300 people actually died as a result of the fire. (No one ever came up with an exact figure as to the number of dead.) But over 90,000 people were homeless. Martial law was declared, and Lieutenant General Philip Sheridan (of Civil War fame) was put in charge of the city.

Although the fire fighting was at an end, the 90,000 homeless people had to be fed. Safe drinking water had to be found, as well as clothing and shelter arranged. A horrified country sent help to Chicago by the trainload. And Chicago immediately set about rebuilding from the ashes. New buildings grew tall and even more people came to the "Windy City." By 1880, few scars were left of the fire of 1871.

Who has not heard of Mrs. O'Leary's cow and the Chicago fire? News of that city's disaster traveled quickly around the world. Yet not far away in Peshtigo, Wisconsin, another fire raged on the same day which killed 1,500 Wisconsin citizens and totally destroyed the town itself.

The forests around Peshtigo were bone dry after a very hot summer and drought. They were ripe for the fire that jumped from tree to tree, gathering in intensity and heat as the wind helped it move across four million acres of timber.

Peshtigo was a town dependent upon the logging industry. The sawmill there produced some 150,000 board feet of lumber in an ordinary day, and most of the 2000 inhabitants lived off the wood of the land. The area which was cleared near the town had a few farms; anyone who had time could go fishing in the Peshtigo River which ran right through town.

This mural, painted on the wall of the Peshtigo Fire Museum, shows the town's residents' flight to the Peshtigo River. More than 1,500 people died in the blaze. The heat from the fire was so intense that it even killed many of those who had already submerged themselves in the river.

Forest fire was the greatest threat to Peshtigo. On Sunday night, October 8, this threat became a reality. At 9 p.m., the church bells rang out a warning to the town. Sparks were already falling and what fire-fighting equipment there was could do little or nothing to stop the spreading flames. The town was tinder—and, like dry tinder, it burned fast.

The townspeople, forced out of burning buildings, headed toward the river. This plan of action, though, offered little safety. On the bridge across the river, two groups of frightened people met—each group hoping to reach safety on the other side. But neither group made it, as the bridge collapsed under the weight of these panic-stricken citizens.

Even those who did manage to reach the river were not safe. Some submerged themselves completely in the water—only to surface when their lungs forced them to come up for air. The heat was so intense that they died instantly.

Peshtigo was not the only town devastated by the fire, although it was by far the hardest hit. Loss of life and property damage occurred in other areas of Wisconsin, too, such as Sugarbush, Williamsville, Manistee, and Glen Haven. Towns in neighboring states were also victim to the blaze.

When the flames died down, Peshtigo was rebuilt. The town is still listed on the map today—and there is a monument there to remind others of the fire that razed Peshtigo over 100 years ago.

When the Tay Bridge was dedicated, Queen Victoria knighted its designer, Thomas Bouch, in a ceremony which took place on the bridge. Spanning the Firth of Tay in Scotland, the bridge had taken seven years to build. Although it was pronounced safe by the Board of Trade inspector, trains traveling the bridge had to keep their speed at 25 miles per hour. The inspector also quietly questioned the effect of a high wind on the bridge. No one heard those quiet remarks.

The Tay Bridge was the longest one in the world at that time. It stood on 85 piers and some of the large spans were 245 feet in length.

Sunday, December 28, was a dark and stormy night. A full gale was blowing up from the sea, when the mail train approached the Tay Bridge. Even the sounds of the train were drowned out in the howling wind. The 75 people onboard were traveling from Edinburgh to Dundee.

The Tay Bridge, over which the train had to travel in its trip from Edinburgh to Dundee, stood on 85 piers. This is a picture of the bridge before its awful collapse.

All things were going according to plan. Tickets had been collected, and the mail train started across. Suddenly, there was a flash of light—darkness followed quickly afterwards. No one on either shore was certain as to what had happened until the light of the moon told them the story.

When the moon came from behind the clouds on that windy night, those watching saw an empty space were the bridge had once stood. It had collapsed into the Tay River, taking the mail train with it.

Without communication, no one on either side of the bridge could tell what had happened. It was hoped that the mail train had made it across the bridge before the collapse. This was proved to be false.

Mailbags were found washed ashore, as were parts of the train's wreckage. A ferry went out to search for survivors; however, the entire train had gone to a watery grave on that awful night.

Amazingly, the engine of the train was ultimately salvaged and managed to continue in service for many years. But that was all that was able to be saved—and nothing could make up for the loss of life.

Although Sir Thomas Bouch, knighted at the opening of the Tay Bridge, was already at work on a bridge across the Firth of Forth, he did not complete that work. His disgrace emerged when the Board of Enquiry stated that the bridge across the Tay had been designed, built, and maintained poorly. The Tay Bridge was less than one year old when it collapsed on that cold and windy December night.

This view from the Dundee end of the Tay Bridge shows what remained when the bridge collapsed and hurled the mail train into the water below.

THE VOLCANIC MONSTER OF SUNDA STRAIT

The island of Krakatoa, located in the Sunda Strait between Java and Sumatra in 1883, was composed of three volcanic cones around a submerged cauldron-shaped basin. Although each volcano had a separate name—the largest of these was called Rakata, while the other two were named Danan and Perbutwatan—the nearby natives called them all by the island's name of Krakatoa.

Originally, Java and Sumatra were joined together like one island. But earthquakes and volcanic eruptions succeeded in dividing the two and leaving Krakatoa's tallest volcano rising from the Sunda Strait between them.

Krakatoa had previously erupted in 1680, but not much is recorded about the incident—except that there were some slight explosions and probably some lava flow. This was then followed by a long period of calm. The sides of the volcano became covered with jungle greenery and abundant with fruit. While no one actually lived on Krakatoa, natives from nearby Java and Sumatra frequently came by boat and climbed the rocks to enjoy the fruits found there.

In the early 19th Century, men of the sea paid little attention to Krakatoa. It was just an island in the East Indies—a lush, green island which housed a very quiet volcano.

Krakatoa remained dormant for 200 years. But, in September of 1880, a few warning shocks were felt. Even though the island was uninhabited, the shocks were noted; however, they alarmed no one.

The German warship *Elizabeth* was cruising near Krakatoa on Sunday, May 20, 1883. Her captain reported a strange vapor cloud hanging over Krakatoa which rose to a height of six to seven miles upward.

This view of Sunda Strait, taken in the 20th Century, shows Krakatoa as it looked before the great eruption of 1883. The volcano had been quiet for 200 years before that fatal August day in 1883.

The cloud, seen from the *Elizabeth,* was composed of ash and pumice spewing forth from the volcano. Within a week, the explosions ceased and calm came once again to the island. However, this calm was only to last a few weeks.

On June 19, new explosions were heard from Krakatoa. Another vapor column rose into the air and the volcano gave off increasingly-dense falling ash. According to one observer, twenty inches of dust covered the island. The brilliant green of the jungle was completely covered with the gray dust. Steam columns and dust were being emitted from almost every volcanic opening on Krakatoa. But once again, things grew quiet on the island.

By August 27, Krakatoa was no longer silent. Four mighty explosions of the volcano, which sounded like violent thunderclaps, echoed through the still air. The sound traveled 1800 miles away to Manila, and it was also heard 1900 miles away in Australia. Even the tiny island of Rodrigues in the Indian Ocean—3000 miles away—heard the roar.

But the sound was only part of the drama of the Sunday explosions. With the third and most violent eruption, a cloud of ash rose 50 miles into the air. Ash and volcanic pumice rained over an area of some 290,000 square miles—bringing the darkness of night to the places where it fell.

The greatest cause of death was still to come. The eruptions at Krakatoa were to plunge the island into the sea, creating huge tidal waves known as tsunami. The tsunami brought tons and tons of water to the low-lying coastlines of Sumatra and Java—both thickly populated. These two areas were totally destroyed. One-hundred and sixty-five villages vanished in the huge tidal wave and 36,000 people were reported lost.

The tidal wave reached a height of 80 feet in some places and 120 feet in others. The underwater shock waves were felt as far away as the English Channel.

Volcanic ash continued to be in the atmosphere for two years, circling the globe and providing outstanding and unusual blood-red sunsets.

As for Krakatoa, the 3,000-foot volcanic island sank into the sea and did not rise again until 1937. In that year, a new cone rose from the sea. This new cone was called ''Anak Krakatoa'' or the ''Child of Krakatoa.'' Today, Anak Krakatoa is a new volcanic island—and active as well.

Man cannot be certain yet, but it is entirely possible that the Sunda Strait may still hold another volcanic monster deep within the bowels of the earth.

''The demon of the Indian Ocean'', as Krakatoa has often been called, erupted in vaporous columns, spewing ash and pumice over an area of approximately 290,000 square miles. The huge tidal waves which followed the eruption were known as ''tsunami.''

THE BLIZZARD OF '88

The headlines which screamed across the front page of the New York Herald on March 13, 1888 were reflections of one of the worst blizzards to hit the northeast section of the United States:

SNOWBOUND
New York's Mighty Pulse
Almost Stilled by a Terrible Storm
Raging Wind and Blinding Drift
The City's Busiest Thoroughfares
Turned Into Scenes of
Winter Desolation

How many people actually saw those headlines in the snow-covered city is unknown, as New York was virtually at a standstill. The recorded snowfall was 20.9 inches and drifts reached as high as the third-story windows of some buildings.

The Saturday before "Blizzard Monday" was a mild, sunny day all up and down the east coast. Birds had started coming back to the north from their winter retreat and farmers had already begun planting their fields. Spring, seemingly, had arrived and, from Maine to Maryland, peole were enjoying it.

This scene at Broadway and 31st Street in New York City shows the 20.9 inches of snow which isolated New York from the rest of the country. Communications with the outside world were at a standstill at the height of the blizzard.

A spring rain which began on Sunday morning turned into a steady downpour by the afternoon. The New York City Weather Bureau was puzzled as to why there were no weather reports coming in from the National Weather Bureau in Washington, D.C. They had no way of knowing that the worst blizzard of the century was moving toward New York from the south. Washington and Baltimore were already buried under the snow.

When New Yorkers awoke on Monday, they still did not realize the extent of the storm to come. They saw their city blanketed in white, with big snowflakes still falling. Despite this, many people went on with their daily routine: some went to work; children were bundled up and sent to school. However, the schools dismissed early and most of the children had to make their way home through drifts taller than they were.

As the day wore on, conditions grew steadily worse. Snow drifts rose to over six feet in some places, while in others they were as high as ten feet. Winds gusted up to 75 miles per hour and New York City, along with other major east-coast cities, was cut off from the rest of the country. Wires were down; fire alarm systems did not work and transportation facilities were useless.

Snow drifts as high as six feet made the digging out quite a chore. As this picture shows, the drifts were taller than a young child.

New Yorkers were forced off of stalled trains and had to walk along the tracks in order to make their way home.

People attempting to get to their homes were in desperate trouble. On Monday, the snow fell so heavily that a man's footprints could be covered in less than five minutes. As the storm continued, those who walked the streets had to fight the large drifts. People were found frozen under the snow when the city dug out later on.

Those trying to reach New York by train were well aware that the snow covered more than the city. Trains were stopped by huge drifts as early as Sunday night and people suffered from cold and lack of food. Help could not reach those trains as the blizzard continued to rage. Many of those who left the trains to try to walk to safety were found dead after the snow had melted.

Even Times Square took some time getting back to normal after the Blizzard of '88. By the Friday after "Blizzard Monday," most vestiges of the storm had melted away and spring returned to New York.

EPILOGUE

By Tuesday morning, the falling snow stopped and the east coast, as well as New York City, began the job of digging out. Stories of death and destruction from the storm were numerous. Reports had it that deaths numbered 400 people or more.

Twenty-two people were drowned at a fishing community in Delaware, as fishing boats and large schooners were tossed by fierce winds and snow gales. Some people died from aftereffects of the storm such as heart attacks or exposure.

Five days after the great blizzard of 1888 struck, spring had returned to the east coast. The snow was a bad memory—perhaps best summed up by the New York Herald's headline of March 14 . . .

A NIGHT OF DEVASTATION

Angry waters swept through Johnstown, Pennsylvania, leaving death and destruction in their wake. Buildings collapsed like match boxes, and people were swept to their death.

Dam On South Fork Creek

The story of the Johnstown Flood actually began many years before May 31, 1889. It began with the building of a series of canals and railways to connect two important Pennsylvania cities—Philadelphia and Pittsburgh.

The traveler going west wanted to get to his destination as quickly as possible—a situation which has not changed very much in recent years.

In those days, people traveled between Johnstown and Pittsburgh—the last leg of the journey west—by barge. Thus, the canal through which they passed required a year-round supply of water to keep it operational.

To provide that steady water supply, engineers built a dam at South Fork Creek in the 1840s.

The dam stood more than 100 feet above the old creek bed, and the flow of water from the lake into the canal was controlled by valves. These valves permitted water to flow out through five outlet pipes. There was also a spillway on one end of the dam.

As time marched on, steam engines gradually replaced the canal barges. By 1854, train travel was completed from Johnstown to Pittsburgh and there was no longer a need for the South Fork Dam.

Lakefront Resort Community

The lake in the Allegheny Mountains no longer offered a commercial need, but the setting was ideal for a resort community. For this reason, a group of wealthy businessmen from Pittsburgh bought the lake and renamed it Conemaugh Lake in 1879. People built homes around the lake and escaped from the hot city for part of every summer. Calling themselves the ''South Fork Fishing and Hunting Club,'' they were a socially-elite and exclusive group.

In 1880, the owners of the Cambria Iron Works of Johnstown were concerned about the safety of the dam itself. They sent an engineer to the site to appraise its condition. The report showed that there was a small break, badly repaired after a storm in 1862, that might cause trouble if the lake filled completely. The report also stated that the discharge pipes had rusted out and there was no way to lower the water level. These factors were considered dangerous in an area where flooding was frequent.

The man wearing a derby was seated on an uprooted tree between two of the houses which were destroyed by the flood waters. More than 2,000 people lost their lives in the devastating flood.

Help was rushed to the victims of the Johnstown flood. Shown here is a temporary Red Cross hotel which was used to house and feed many of the homeless victims.

A copy of the engineer's report was sent to the owners of the lake, but its contents were ignored. The owners stocked the lake with fish and even blocked the end of the dam with nets to prevent their fish from escaping.

By the spring of 1889, most people in and around Johnstown had forgotten the engineer's report. Memorial Day came after a very wet spring—11 inches of rain falling in the month of May. On the night of May 30, eight inches more fell in a matter of hours.

Johnstown, a growing industrial complex, was accustomed to flooding. But the water in the streets of the city on the morning of May 31 showed definite signs of the flood being a bad one. The inhabitants of the area, though, could not even imagine just how big and how devastating this one was going to be. Water was rising at as much as one foot an hour, and the citizens moved to higher ground by rowboat.

The lake was overflowing from all the rain, and water poured over the top of the dam. At 12 p.m., huge sheets of water exerted their full force on the dam itself. By 3 p.m., a 300-foot section of the dam wall burst, releasing a wall of water as high as 40 feet.

The angry water rushed down the valley carrying uprooted trees and huge rocks with it. An entire farm with all its buildings was swept away as well. The village of South Fork was inundated and its cluster of houses swept away. Mineral Point and East Conemaugh disappeared. A stranded passenger train was covered by huge sheets of water.

People were overcome by the fast-moving water before they knew what was upon them. Houses floated along with people clinging to the roofs; when their strength gave out, they were pulled into the water to drown.

By the time the flood water hit Johnstown, it was more than just a wall of water. Tons of rubble, including wood, iron, stone, uprooted trees and dead bodies were being pulled along. Much of this debris piled up in a mountainous mass at the site of Stone Bridge. Here was the final horror. Fire broke out and the mass of burning debris killed even more people; it was as if they had stepped into a huge furnace.

The stories which appeared in the newspapers after the flood told of horror after horror. Husbands watched as their entire families sank into the water; children were orphaned by the score. There was just no end to the dead. The tales were grizzly but true. More than 2,000 people lost their lives in the Johnstown Flood on that day in May—the day the dam burst.

Although the cry—REMEMBER THE *MAINE*—was heard throughout the country at the beginning of the Spanish-American War, there is no certainty that the battleship U.S.S. *Maine* was sunk by enemies of the United States. The explosion of the *Maine* was, however, an emotional issue which helped launch our country into that war.

In February of 1898, many American citizens were living in Cuba. At that time, Cuba had been fighting Spain's interests in it for three years. Riots were common in the streets of Havana, and this seemed to be ample reason for the United States to protect the Americans who were there.

When the Navy sent the battleship U.S.S. *Maine* to the port of Havana, its purpose was to be alert to the needs of the United States citizens. The *Maine* was to offer protection for those citizens should they require it. This was not in any way a wartime maneuver.

The U.S.S. Maine lay at anchor in Havana harbor loaded with explosives and ammunition. The battleship, under the command of Captain Charles D. Ligsbee, was in Cuba to protect American citizens against the riots in Havana.

The explosion which took place at 9:45 p.m. on February 15 destroyed the Maine and took the lives of 250 crewmen. A torn and battered hull was all that remained of the once-proud ship.

The *Maine*, being a battleship, carried huge guns and torpedoes—not to mention a crew of 250 who manned the decks.

For nearly three weeks, the *Maine* was anchored in the harbor at Havana. All was quiet and the Navy's watchdog was simply waiting in the event of some untoward action of the Cubans or Spanish.

On the evening of February 15, peace and quiet was rudely interrupted. At 9:45 p.m., an explosion took place which was heard for miles around. Those on the shore saw columns of black smoke—quickly followed by shooting flames—rising from where the *Maine* had once been. In a matter of minutes, the U.S.S. *Maine* was destroyed and all hands aboard her killed in the explosion. Two-hundred-and-fifty men died instantly with no chance of being saved.

The World, a New York newspaper owned by Joseph Pulitzer, was the first to get out a report on the sinking of the battleship. The cable sent by *World* reporters to New York was written in Spanish so it would not have to be translated and approved by any censor's office.

A headline from *The World* on February 17 shows that there was an area of doubt as to how the *Maine* had been destroyed. The newspaper headline read:

Maine explosion caused by bomb or torpedo?

One of *The World*'s rivals was the *New York Journal.* The *Journal*'s headline was a statement, not a question. This paper's headline read:

Destruction of the War Ship *Maine* was the work of an enemy.

The *Journal* offered a $50,000 reward for "the conviction of the criminals" who were supposed to have sent the *Maine* to a watery grave.

Emotions ran high in the United States as a result of the sinking of the *Maine*. Politicians and citizens alike were inclined to believe that the sinking was the result of sabotage. However, facts revealed later on do not conclusively support this theory.

President McKinley gave what we now call a press release to *The World* shortly before midnight on February 17.

"Based upon information now in his possession, the President believes that the *Maine* was blown up as the result of an accident, and he hopes the Court of Inquiry will develop that fact. If it is found that the disaster was not an accident, prompt and decisive steps will be taken in the premises."

No one could prove that there was any sabotage on the *Maine*. Rather, those who curbed their emotions and were actually looking for proof were inclined to believe that some of the mighty explosives carried by the *Maine* had simply blown up.

Despite the absence of proof of guilt from Spain, the majority of people at home in the United States continued to believe that the *Maine* had been a victim of war. Assistant Secretary Theodore Roosevelt, who was later to lead forces up San Juan Hill in Cuba, believed the explosion of the *Maine* was not an accident. The newspapers around the country helped to give credence to this belief.

The sinking of the *Maine* was not a war-related disaster. Cooler heads declared much later that the explosion was caused by the torpedoes and ammunition which were on board the battleship. However, the United States was ripe for war—and the explosion of the *Maine* was all that was needed to launch the United States int a war with Spain on April 25, 1898.

The sinking of the Maine was not a war-related disaster, although many accused foreign countries of sabotage. The actual cause of the explosion was ultimately attributed to the torpedoes and ammunition which were on board the ship at the time.

Doomsday at St. Pierre

Hero on a Burning Stage

140 Acres of Destruction

The Day that Frisco Shook

Eighteen Minutes of Flaming Horror

SOS for the Unsinkable Titanic

Death at the Docks of Chicago

Flanders Grippe, La Grippe, Blitz Katarrh, Spanish Flu

The Great Molasses Flood

Tokyo and Yokohama Devastated

St. Francis Dam — Where None Survived

The Sinking of the Vestris

The Great British Airship, R101

Flood Waters of the Mighty Yangtse River

Dirigible Akron Crash at Sea

The Ship that was Burned Out

"Wet" Gas Causes School Explosion

Flames From the Sky at Lakehurst, New Jersey

Hurricane Sweeps New England

Fire at the Cocoanut Grove

The Burning of the Big Top

Gas Tanks Explode at East Side Gas Co.

Explosion at Texas City, Texas

Five-Day Floods on Honshu Island

Earthquake at Ecuador

When the Big Muddy Burst its Banks

The Death Throes of the U.S.S. Hobson

The Auckland Express at Tangiwai Bridge

Andrea Doria

A Christmas Shopping Nightmare

This picture of Mt. Pelée at peace shows the difficult terraine in the area of Martinique. Citizens of St. Pierre, the French colony situated below the volcano, ignored the early rumblings of Mt. Pelée.

St. Pierre, nicknamed the Paris of the West Indies, was located five miles below Mount Pelée in the French colony of Martinique. The basis of the island's economy was sugar, rum, and bananas—and the 30,000 inhabitants of St. Pierre enjoyed a free and easy way of life.

Although they lived in the shadow of Mount Pelée, the people of Martinique were not afraid of the great volcano. The main crater of Pelée held a beautiful lake, and many enjoyed going there for picnics. St. Pierre itself was considered a very pleasant place, although the city was a contrast in great wealth and extreme poverty. By the day's end on May 8, 1902, not many people would live to describe what St. Pierre had once been.

Early in April, Mount Pelée began to steam and expand, but nearby inhabitants took little or no notice of this. Since an erupting volcano was bad for the tourist business, the volcanic activity was played down. Mount Pelée, however, refused to be quiet. The rumblings continued and, at the end of April, the mountain gave forth a shower of ashes which covered an area for miles around—including the town of St. Pierre. The heavy ash was killing wildlife on the mountainside; a heavy sulphuric smell hung over the town. Yet, people still refused to be alarmed.

Shortly after the eruption on May 8, the volcano spewed forth a tower of black, glass-like rock which was called "Pelée's Spine."
It reached to a height of nearly 1,000 feet.

The French newspaper, *Les Colonies,* wrote soothing editorials to quiet any public unrest—and they were successful, too, since the people believed them. Even the governor of the island refused to consider the possibility of danger. He ordered troops into St. Pierre to prevent townspeople from leaving the area, hoping thus to avert a widespread panic. By his actions, though, the governor entombed the entire city when disaster came.

Early on the morning of May 8, Mount Pelée burst forth with flames and smoke. The time recorded on the military hospital clock—which somehow remained in-

tact—was 7:52 a.m. In a matter of minutes, the town of St. Pierre was demolished.

Aboard the passenger ship S.S. *Roraima,* Assistant Purser Thompson lived to tell the tale of Pelée's violent discharge. The *Roraima* had entered the port of St. Pierre early in the morning and was one of the two ships not totally destroyed by the eruption. Thompson later described the horror that he saw.

"There was no warning. The side of the volcano was ripped out and there hurled towards us a solid wall of flame. It sounded like a thousand cannons. The wave of

A child looks down on all that remained of St. Pierre after the violent explosion of Mt. Pelee. The entire city was demolished.

fire was on us and over us like a lightning flash, a hurricane of fire which rolled in a mass straight down on St. Pierre. . .''

The fire, gasses, and steam which spewed out of the mountaintop moved with incredible speed. Thousands died from just one breath of the fiery whirlpool; it was so hot that lungs were shriveled in an instant. People had their clothes burned off of them and died with the sound of the mountain's thundering noise ringing in their ears.

When the fire reached the harbor, it continued its destruction. Men standing on the decks of ships became torches; the ships themselves burned like kindling. A huge tidal wave, caused by the eruption, capsized and damaged the floating vessels. The water around the stricken ships was a boiling cauldron, sending up great clouds of steam.

Unlike the eruption of Mount Vesuvius in A.D. 79, the Mount Pelée explosion did not have much lava flow. The terrible damage was caused by the extremely hot steam and noxious gases which enveloped the town of St. Pierre.

While St. Pierre was devastated, the great mountain above was not finished. On May 20, an earthquake shook the island, killing even more people throughout Martinique and destroying neighboring villages on the mountainside.

For two months after Pelée's eruption in early May, a spectacular sight could be seen from the center cone of the volcano. A ''spine'' of lava rose into the air at a height of more than 1,000 feet to form a towering mass of hardened lava. Some called this the ''Tower of Pelée.'' It disintegrated, though, before a year had passed.

St. Pierre did rebuild its town— but it never again became the community it had once been. Less than 7,000 lived where once there were over 30,000. The free and easy life of a tourist colony had ended in a hurricane of fire and a cloud of ash on May 8, 1902.

All that remained of the American Consulate in St. Pierre was a wall and debris. What had once been a thriving city for tourists never again rose to the heights it had once known before the volcano's violent eruption.

HERO ON A BURNING STAGE

Eddie Foy, Sr. was indeed a hero on the burning stage of the Wednesday matinee performance of "Bluebeard" at the Iroquois Theatre in Chicago. Despite his heroic efforts, though, the death toll exceeded 600 people before the day was over. But panic, not fire, was the cause.

The Iroquois Theatre was one of Chicago's finest and newest theatres; it was listed on the playbill as "fireproof."

On the fatal afternoon, the Iroquois was packed with patrons. Later estimates said there were 2,000 people inside, although there were only enough seats for 1,600. An untold number of tickets were sold to standees.

The Iroquois Theatre, one of Chicago's finest and newest, caught fire in a matter of minutes during the second act of the musical farce, "Bluebeard." The well-known actor, Eddie Foy, Sr., attempted to calm a panicking audience. Despite his efforts, the death toll exceeded 600 people.

When the firemen were able to get into the burning theatre, they found that many victims died of panic as well as from the actual flames. Over 200 of the dead were children who had come to view the performance.

Many of those who came were not only interested in the program, but in the theatre itself. The Iroquois had a huge promenade and foyer. There was lavish use of heavy, plush draperies and plate glass. The distance from floor to ceiling was 60 feet, with vast staircases leading to the mezzanine and balcony. It was indeed a showcase of elegance.

The musical farce, "Bluebeard," an import from Drury Lane in London, was a play admirably suited to children. Much of the audience consisted of families or mothers with their children, all celebrating the end of the Christmas holidays. The first act of the play proceeded without incident, and the spectators were having a delightful time.

When the second act began, a double octet, composed of eight men and eight women, was on stage singing "In the Pale Moonlight." The effect of a moonlit night was created by blue arc lights playing on gauze draperies and backdrops. Suddenly, one of the arc lights set fire to the gauze.

Had the Iroquois truly been fireproof, a nearby extinguisher might have put out what started as a very minor flame. However, the man handling the light used an inefficient fire extinguisher with no results. The gauze, which was quick to ignite, lit other material. The fire began to spread.

Although there was a firehouse near the theatre, there was no telephone with which to call. A stagehand ran to the firehouse to put in the alarm. Firemen with hoses were on the scene within two minutes.

Inside the theatre, more and more people became aware of the spreading flames. Eddie Foy, who was still in his dressing room, heard the cries of "Fire!" In costume, he raced to his son and gave the child to someone to take out of the theatre. That child, in later years, described the event by saying:

"He picked me up and threw me over the heads of other people to a man who got me out of there."

Once the safety of his child was assured, Eddie Foy returned to the stage. Here, he commanded what remained of the orchestra to play something loud, while he attempted to calm a frightened crowd. He tried to reassure the people who could hear him and is credited with saving an untold number of lives with his directions.

But despite the bravery of Eddie Foy, people began to panic. What was supposed to have been an asbestos curtain was lowered. However, the curtain only went down halfway and succeeded in creating a draft which blew from the open back doors of the theatre into the main part of the theatre itself.

Mothers and children became separated in the stampede for exits. There were actually thirty different exits at the Iroquois, but many of them were covered with plush draperies and some were even locked. None were marked. Pile-ups of people clawing at each other occurred wherever there was a possible exit. Fire fighters later found people with heel marks stamped into their flesh by the living who had walked over the fallen.

The actual fire was under control in less than ten minutes. None of the dead were killed by flames, but many died from smoke inhalation, the extreme heat of the burning building, and the panic which ensued.

The terrible fire at the Iroquois Theatre was given wide publicity all over the United States. One estimate said that within a matter of days, some 50 theatres were closed as being fire hazards. In fact, statutes were soon passed to insure proper precautions against fire in all public buildings. Although this was one benefit of the Iroquois fire, it is somewhat like closing the barn door after the horse has run away.

This picture of the stage in back of the proscenium arch shows what remained after the fire was brought under control.

140 ACRES OF DESTRUCTION

The automatic fire alarm in the basement of the John E. Hurst and Company building rang persistently at 10:48 a.m. in the cold, clear Sunday morning of February 7. The Hurst Building, in Baltimore, Maryland, was a six story, wholesale dry goods warehouse located in the heart of the downtown business district.

The Baltimore Fire Department was quick to respond to the alarm, and Engine 15, a steam pumper and a hose wagon, rushed to the scene. The fire was ahead of them, though.

The entire Hurst Building, loaded with piles of dry goods, seemed to explode and was shortly ablaze from cellar to roof. Windows on the upper floors of the building were blown out by the force of the explosion, as were the windows in neighboring buildings. The blaze, which began as a small, one-alarm fire, was able to leap from building to building in the crowded downtown area of the city. One-hundred-and-forty acres were soon to be burned out.

The Baltimore Fire of 1904 caused no loss of life, but 140 acres were destroyed. This view of Fayette and Guilford Avenues shows the burned-out shells of some buildings which remained standing. The building at the far right is Baltimore's City Hall.

The fire chief called to the scene was George W. Horton, and he set about to direct the fire-fighting activities. He soon recognized the awful possibilities in store and ordered out all available equipment and men. However, within a short time of the fire's start, Chief Horton incurred injuries from a falling electric wire and had to be taken to a nearby hospital. Command of the fire now fell to others.

Most of the fire fighters, though not many of the spectators, realized that the Baltimore Fire was blazing out of control. Requests for help were sent to the nearby cities of Washington, Philadelphia, New York, and Wilmington. Washington sent equipment and men by train in less than two hours. Other cities, both large and small, sent in the same as quickly as they could.

Despite the arrival of fire-fighting equipment, the flames continued to grow. One problem which none had foreseen was the lack of standardization of fire equipment. Hoses and couplings were not uniform and so did not fit Baltimore hydrants. But with the rapidity of the spreading flames and the 20 to 30 mile-per-hour winds, it is doubtful that much could have been saved even with uniform fittings.

Finally, those in charge decided to try dynamite to halt the conflagration. Many structures were demolished by the blasts, but this did little to halt the fire.

The *Baltimore Sun* Newspaper Building was one of the first iron buildings to be erected in America. The building went up in flames, leaving only four pillars standing. *Sun* reporters, however, continued to work to cover the story, as did the other two newspapers in town.

The fire raged unchecked all through Sunday and into Monday, February 8. Not until the fire reached Jones Falls, a small river running through the east end of city, was it possible for firemen to get the blaze und control. The 50 foot canal of Jones Falls served as an adequate firebreak to stop the fire. The out-of-town fire engines worked here, drawing water directly from this oasis. Finally the flames died.

Although 140 acres were burned to the ground and there were millions of dollars of damage to the city, the Baltimore Fire did not claim any lives. Along with Chief Horton, some 40 firemen suffered injuries of one kind or another.

Baltimore had much to be grateful for after the fire. Only ''things'' had been lost to the flames—not lives. The city began rebuilding immediately. In a comparatively short time, a new Baltimore emerged from the ashes of 1904.

The fire, which raged unchecked for two days, left piles of debris and charred-building remains as its mark. Equipment and help were rushed to the city from as far away as New York.

51

THE DAY THAT FRISCO SHOOK

52

April 18, 1906

San Francisco is a city accustomed to earthquakes. The city sits atop the San Andreas fault and within a short distance of the Hayward fault. It is these faults which occasionally cause a shift in the earth's surface—known to man as earthquakes.

Lesser earthquakes had been felt in San Francisco toward the end of the 19th Century, but these had done little damage. In no way did they prepare the citizens for what was to occur on Wednesday, April 18, 1906.

San Francisco had grown from the rowdy city it had been during the 1849 gold rush to a more cosmopolitan place in 1906. Nob Hill sported the elegant homes of the very wealthy. People flocked to the Palace Hotel, the Barbary Coast and, of course, Chinatown. The city was indeed a cultural melting pot, with a population reaching approximately 450,000.

Buckled curbstones and pavements showed the effects of the earthquake that shook San Francisco in 1906. This was the scene at Lexington Street and the corner of 18th Street after the quake.

On Tuesday, April 17, fashionable San Francisco was to celebrate the performance of the Metropolitan Opera company. The great Caruso himself was playing Don Jose in the opera "Carmen." Society welcomed the event with gala parties, music, dancing, and drinking. The next morning, however, these very same revelers would awake to find the world around them shaking uncontrollably.

The first shock of the earthquake was felt at 5:12 a.m. Many woke up to the sounds of rumbling and muffled roars filling the air. Some were actually thrown out of their beds, their possessions tumbling down around them. The earth was rocking back and forth. The first shock lasted about thirty seconds. Then followed ten seconds of complete silence, as if the world was at a standstill. A second tremor lasted for another 25 seconds.

Enrico Caruso was asleep in his room at the Palace Hotel when the quake began. He is said to have sung a few bars of music through an open window before making his way down into the street. Once there, he sat on his suitcase until others helped him to a place of safety. It is said that he swore never to return to San Francisco.

The shocks of the earthquake left the city in shambles. Only the dome of the newly-built City Hall, said to be indestructible, remained standing. Mansions on Nob Hill were reduced to rubble, and other houses in the city stood at rakish angles one to another. While the worst property damage from the quake was in the downtown area, the loss of life was comparatively small. Some people had indeed been crushed in and under the falling buildings, but the early hour of the day prevented death from taking a larger toll. Unfortunately, fire was to do what the earthquake had not done—and it broke out all over the city.

In their rush to get out from under falling debris, people had left heaters burning. But worse than this, the earthquake had broken gas mains and water mains.

The dome of City Hall and some of its walls remained standing after the earthquake and fire which followed.

Streets were impassable with open fissures and buckling. There was little or no way to fight the fires which were continually erupting all over town.

Months before the earthquake and fire, Fire Chief Danny Sullivan had declared the city of San Francisco impossible to protect in the case of a major blaze. The fires which started after the quake proved the fire chief to be correct. There was not even water available to quench the consuming flames.

The fire, fanned by a stiff breeze, burned out of control for three long days. There were no means of controlling the conflagration. Attempts were made to dynamite whole streets in an effort to create firebreaks and stop the flames from spreading. These attempts, though, proved fruitless.

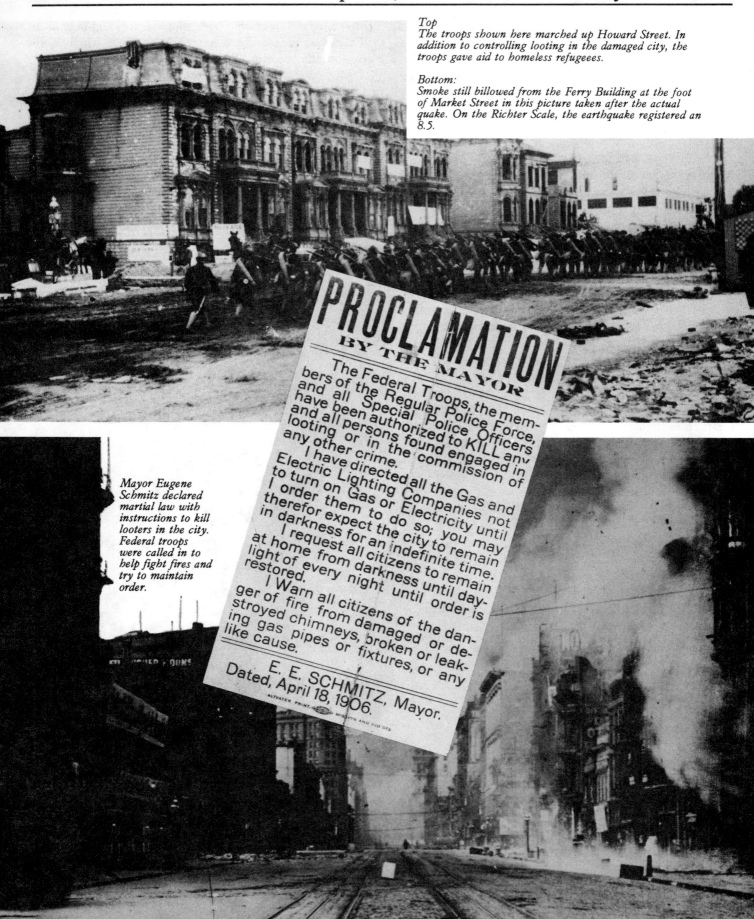

Top
The troops shown here marched up Howard Street. In addition to controlling looting in the damaged city, the troops gave aid to homeless refugeees.

Bottom:
Smoke still billowed from the Ferry Building at the foot of Market Street in this picture taken after the actual quake. On the Richter Scale, the earthquake registered an 8.5.

Mayor Eugene Schmitz declared martial law with instructions to kill looters in the city. Federal troops were called in to help fight fires and try to maintain order.

PROCLAMATION
BY THE MAYOR

The Federal Troops, the members of the Regular Police Force, and all Special Police Officers have been authorized to KILL any and all persons found engaged in looting or in the commission of any other crime.

I have directed all the Gas and Electric Lighting Companies not to turn on Gas or Electricity until I order them to do so; you may therefor expect the city to remain in darkness for an indefinite time.

I request all citizens to remain at home from darkness until daylight of every night until order is restored.

I Warn all citizens of the danger of fire from damaged or destroyed chimneys, broken or leaking gas pipes or fixtures, or any like cause.

E. E. SCHMITZ, Mayor.
Dated, April 18, 1906.

Looting occurred in some places and Mayor Eugene Schmitz ordered martial law. Federal troops came to help fight the fires and maintain order. The mayor decreed that troops should kill anybody found looting. A curfew was enforced to clear the streets until daylight. San Francisco was indeed a disaster area.

When daylight came on Saturday, some light rain came with it which was enough to dampen the flames. The city could now take time to look at itself. There were four square miles of devastation. Five-hundred-and-fourteen city blocks—containing more than 28,000 buildings—had been destroyed. The force of the earthquake was recorded at 8.5 on the Richter Scale.

There are only estimates as to the actual number of people killed, ranging from 400 to 1,000.

Residential areas as well as the downtown areas felt the effects of the earthquake. The people in this picture were at least able to get back into their homes, even though all they found inside was debris.

The Triangle Shirtwaist Company was housed on the eighth, ninth, and tenth floors of the Asch Building on the corner of New York's Washington Place and Greene Street. This was the factory where so many of the fashionable shirtwaist dresses of the day were made.

Working conditions in the building were very poor. Rows and rows of sewing machines were set up in very close quarters, and the girls who worked them spent hours in the same back-breaking position. Not many of these girls were able to afford any of the garments which they made. They worked six days a week in airless rooms for a salary of about $5 a week. These were the sweatshops of New York City.

The girls who worked at Triangle came in and went out through very narrow corridors—so narrow that only one person could pass through at a time. This was done so that each girl could be checked as she left the shop to make sure she was not pilfering. Stairways were blocked at points for much the same reason. The owners of the Triangle Shirtwaist Company were very concerned with theft. Had they been more concerned with good working conditions, 145 people might not have died on that Saturday afternoon in 1911.

The time was 4:45 p.m., shortly before quitting time. Many of the employees were either on their way out or preparing to leave when fire broke out on the 8th floor.

The fire started in a pile of scraps under a cutting table. Bins of trash, scraps, and stacks of material were piled high all around the room. Some young women were still working at their sewing machines when the first flames were spotted. Despite the efforts of several of the men, nothing could halt the progress of the flames. Soon, there was pandemonium all around.

The corner of Washington Place and Greene Streets in New York City was the scene of the Triangle Shirtwaist Company's devastating fire. This exterior shot of the building shows the inability of the firemen to reach the upper floors where the fire raged.

The narrow passageways to the outer halls not only prevented stealing from the Triangle Shirtwaist Company, but they also prevented the frightened girls from making their way to safety. The stairways, narrow as well and blocked at points by locked doors, had the girls pushing into one another in vain attempts to open them. The flames cackled at their backs.

This burned-out workroom of the factory was all that remained of the rows of sewing machines and the girls who worked them. The fire claimed the lives of 145 people.

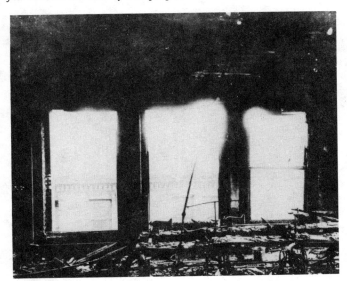

Only one of the three elevators in the building worked and had a maximum capacity of 12 people. Those girls who were near the working elevator crushed into it and closed the door. Many of those left standing there threw themselves on top of the car, dying as they fell.

Some people were lucky and escaped the fire by going to the roof of the building. Once up there, they were able to walk across to a neighboring building and to safety.

Others, not so fortunate, simply broke windows and jumped to their deaths. Those on the ground could never forget the thud of those falling bodies. The building's flimsy fire escapes broke under the weight of all the people trying to use them.

Although the fire department was on the scene, they were practically helpless. Neither the ladders of the fire

The fire escapes at the back of the building were not strong enough to hold the amount of people. Twenty employees fell to their deaths when the flimsy fire escapes collapsed.

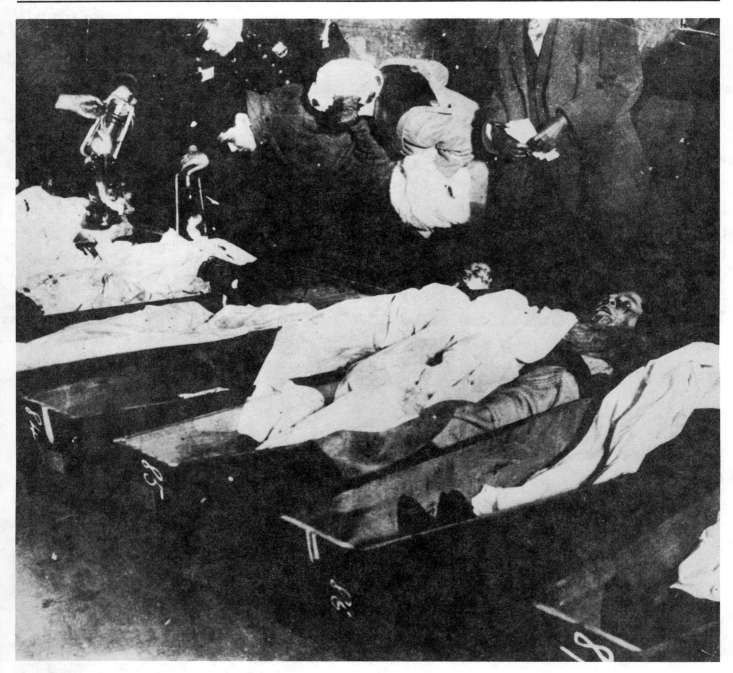

Identification of the victims was difficult. Many were burned beyond recognition.

companies nor their hoses reached up as high as the eighth floor. Even the safety nets which were stretched out on the ground could not catch the bodies as they fell.

In just eighteen minutes, the fire at the Triangle Shirt-waist Company took the lives of 145 people. The building was completely gutted. More than 40 people had jumped from the windows, at least 20 had jumped into the elevator shaft, and more were burned up inside.

EPILOGUE

The men and women who died in the fire were not to be forgotten. As a result of this tragedy, the International Ladies Garment Workers Union became a strong working force to change conditions in the New York City sweat-shops. Ultimately, the state outlawed these hated sweatshops and fire regulations were more strictly enforced.

SOS FOR THE UNSINKABLE TITANIC

Maiden Voyage
First and Last

Great Britain and the White Star Line were justifiably proud of the *Titanic* when she sailed out of Southampton on April 10, 1912. The great ship measured 900 feet long and weighed 66,000 tons. Her maiden voyage was planned to end in New York. But, on her fourth day out at sea, the luxury liner went down.

The *Titanic* was considered unsinkable. It was divided into 16 watertight compartments and was equipped with a double bottom to insure further safety.

The 1,316 passengers on board the ship were not so much concerned with its durability, though. They took this fact for granted. And so did the 885 members of the crew who served them. Since the *Titanic* was supposed to be unsinkable, the men and women who were on board planned to enjoy the ocean crossing to the fullest.

The Titanic, shown in this picture, was considered to be unsinkable. The ship was divided into 16 watertight compartments and equipped with a double bottom to insure further safety.

There were dances and full-dress dinners for the first-class passengers. Among those traveling in this class were some of the most prominent men and women in American society: John Jacob Astor and his wife, Frank Millet, and Benjamin Guggenheim—just to name a few—were on board for the ship's maiden voyage. Also on board was Joseph Bruce Ismay, president of the company which owned the *Titanic*.

By Sunday, April 14, the huge liner was already in open sea. The ship's radio operator, John Phillips, was busy sending messages to Cape Race announcing the time of the *Titanic*'s arrival in New York. Phillips was

This interior view of the Titanic shows the elegance of the restaurant reception room. The ship's passenger list included some of the most prominent men and women in American society.

also receiving messages from other ships in the area warning of unusual icebergs sighted along the route which the *Titanic* was to take.

When Captain Edward Smith was given these warnings, he doubled the iceberg watch. But the *Titanic* continued on her way at top speed.

The night of April 14 was calm and moonless. Suddenly, the crew member on watch shouted that an iceberg was spotted just 500 yards ahead (icebergs were usually sited from a distance of three miles away). The *Titanic,* traveling at a speed of 22 knots, crashed into the iceberg; a 300-foot wound was gouged out of her hull.

Most of the passengers were already in bed when the *Titanic* struck ice. Few of them realized that anything had happened, as the great ship only gave a slight shudder on impact. But Captain Smith knew that the *Titanic* was doomed. The gash in the ship's hull was allowing tons of icy water to pour into the ship's watertight compartments.

Captain Smith ordered Phillips (the radio operator) to send out an SOS distress call. He also ordered the lifeboats to be uncovered. Stewards rushed down the ship's

corridors, knocking on every door of the sleeping passengers' rooms. People were instructed to put on warm clothes and come out on deck. Many of them still did not realize that they were in desperate straits.

Although the crewmen did hasten to uncover the lifeboats, one fact was revealed in later inquiries of the disaster. The total lifeboat capacity on the *Titanic* was for 1,178 people. The ship carried 1,316 passengers on this maiden voyage.

The cry went out among the men on board to allow women and children to get off the sinking ship first. Stories of heroism were told by survivors later on. One wealthy woman, who refused to leave her husband behind, died with him in the icy waters. Stories of cowardice also came to light later on. Some men pushed aside others in their eagerness to climb into the lifeboats.

While the boats were being lowered into the sea below, a band of ship's musicians played the hymn ''Nearer My God to Thee.'' Those who could hear the music joined in and sang.

Many of the third-class passengers were unable to get up on deck. It seemed as if the class distinction also ap-

The Titanic sunk after striking an iceberg in the open sea on her way from Southampton, England, to New York. This is an artist's rendering of the way it happened.

One of the first rescue ships to arrive on the scene was the Carpathia. Here, a boatload of survivors were helped aboard her to safety.

The scene in front of the White Star Line office was total confusion, as anxious relatives and friends waited for word as to which passengers survived the disaster.

plied to the lifeboats; those below went down with the ship.

Captain Smith's final action was to order all to abandon ship. Those who were fortunate enough to be in lifeboats saw the sinking of the *Titanic* before their very eyes. Fifteen-hundred-and-three people went down with the ship.

The action of the radio operator, who remained at his post until the end, saved many of those in the lifeboats. His call for help brought nearby ships to the rescue. One of the closest and first to arrive was the *Carpathia*. She picked up over 600 people from out of the sea and carried them safely back to New York.

EPILOGUE

The entire story of the *Titanic* was not released until after the survivors reached port. Anxious relatives on shore did not know of the life or death of their loved ones for four long days.

While Boards of Inquiry were held in England and the United States after the *Titanic* sank, nothing could change what had happened. In the tradition of the sea, Captain Edward Smith went down with his ship.

DEATH AT THE DOCKS OF CHICAGO

July 24, 1915

63

The Eastland, an excursion steamer, capsized at the dock in the Chicago River and settled in 18 feet of water. More than 2,000 people were aboard at the time.

Early in the morning on Saturday, July 24, the *Eastland,* an excursion packet, was readying herself for a gala trip from the docks of Chicago to Michigan City, Indiana. There, the happy passengers were to enjoy a picnic before returning to Chicago. The all-day trip was planned for the employees and their families of The Western Electric Company; 5,000 people had signed up to go.

Five steamers, including the *Eastland,* were needed to accommodate the expected crowds. This was to be a wonderful outing for all. Unfortunately, it did not work out that way.

The *Eastland* had been completed in 1902, but the ship did not live up to the expectations of her owners. She seemed to be a bit top heavy; in fact, on one early excursion trip, there was a definite list to the starboard. Passengers were ordered to the other side to better distribute the weight. This, in turn, caused a list to port. However, the big steamer settled down and nothing more happened at this time.

In 1907, certain changes were made on the top deck to correct the *Eastland's* instability. At the same time, the boilers were rebuilt to increase the steam pressure. The *Eastland* was then pronounced fit by her owners and continued to travel as an excursion liner on the Great Lakes.

On July 24, the passengers began to arrive at the Clark Street Pier on the Chicago River by 6:30 a.m. The day was not clear and the skies offered the possibility of rain, but this did not dampen the spirits of the employees and their families. They came bearing picnic baskets and other assorted paraphernalia needed for an all-day outing.

For some unknown reason, people kept boarding the *Eastland,* although there were two other steamers on either side of her. More than 2,000 people walked up the ship's gangplank.

Before 7 a.m., Joseph M. Erickson, the chief engineer, observed that the ship was listing to port. Many of the passengers were crowded on the port rail to watch the later passengers come on board. Erickson ordered the opening of a ballast tank to compensate for the listing. However, this did little to correct the problem.

Passengers were then asked to move to starboard, but this request was ignored. They had no idea how critical the situation was to become. People continued to pour on to the already overloaded ship.

By 7:20 a.m., everyone was aware that the *Eastland* was in trouble. The listing to port had not been corrected In a matter of minutes, the 2,000 ton, steel-hulled ship had completely capsized beside the pier. Those who had been waving to others on the port side of the ship were under the water as the *Eastland* turned over onto her side.

Death from drowning came instantly to many who were trapped. Those on the starboard side of the vessel had a better chance for survival. Some managed to walk across the starboard exterior hull, although this proved to be a slippery way to safety. One of the nearby boats tried to shovel ashes onto the exposed hull to help survivors walk across. Although it did help some people, others still lost their footing and their lives in the water by the pier.

Some who were trapped inside the *Eastland* lived to tell about it. Workmen with acetylene torches cut holes in the *Eastland*'s exposed hull to allow the living trapped inside to get out. A small number of people were saved in this way.

Over 800 dead were taken from the ship and the water around her. The death toll, which occurred in a matter of minutes, was shocking. Although help arrived instantly from nearby ships, police, and firemen, the *Eastland* had capsized so quickly that there was nothing to be done for many—except to set up a temporary morgue where the dead could be identified.

Death from drowning came to many of the passengers who were trapped inside. Here, rescue workers are shown recovering bodies from the overturned vessel.

Captain Harry Pedersen, as well as the *Eastland*'s chief engineer and officials of the steamship line, were all indicted for manslaughter and negligence. Their subsequent trial was held in February of 1916 with the renowned Clarence Darrow acting as defense attorney. Darrow's brilliant defense allowed Captain Pedersen to walk away a free man.

Although the Eastland was never again an excursion day liner, she was subsequently sold to the United States Navy and used as a training ship until 1946.

EPILOGUE

As for the *Eastland,* her days as an excursion ship were over. She was subsequently sold to the United States Navy and used as a training ship until 1946. Then, she was taken to a scrap yard very near the same dock where she had capsized in 1915.

In 1918, much of the world was engaged in what was thought to be the "war to end all wars." But, in that same year, a killer was loosed on the world whose equal has rarely been seen. Known throughout most of the English-speaking world as the "Spanish Flu," the disease killed over 20 million people.

Fort Riley, Kansas was one of the first places where influenza showed itself in epidemic proportions. It was March of 1918 when the flu outbreak at Fort Riley made 1,100 men ill and killed 46. At first, the cause of death was listed by the doctors as pneumonia. Later reflections on the progress of the epidemic indicated that it was really the flu.

Since the United States had now entered the war, there were camps of soldiers being readied for overseas service throughout the country. These camps were soon victimized by the flu, as were the Navy's ships. Indeed, even those serving time in California's San Quentin Prison were afflicted with the disease. Five hundred prisoners became ill and three died.

While this was happening in the United States wherever great crowds of people were confined to one area, word of the disease came from overseas. Doughboys already in France had what the French called "la grippe." British Tommies suffered from what their doctors labelled as "Flanders grippe." Scotland, too, was recording regular deaths from the disease.

Berlin reported 160,000 residents contracted what German doctors labelled "Blitz Katarrh." There were reports of the flu from almost every part of the world. However, when the flu hit Spain, the name "Spanish Flu" stuck.

What exactly was the disease? It began with symptoms of sneezing, sniffles, and an awful achiness all over the body. A high fever was part of the illness, and most of the medical community agreed that it was some kind of upper respiratory infection. That the flu was highly contagious is shown by the way it traveled through whole communities of people. However, those living on farms were victims of the epidemic as well as those in more congested areas.

Remedies to cure the disease were almost barbaric. As the doctors could not agree on what the disease was, they could not agree on how to cure it. It seemed to be a matter of luck whether a patient lived or died. However, some of the flu remedies prescribed make interesting reading.

One of the most popular remedies was to cut up an onion, wrap it in a white cloth, and apply it to the chest. It might have cleared the sinuses, but it certainly did not cure the flu.

One doctor prescribed towels soaked in hot vinegar and applied to the abdomen. Frightened people were willing to try almost anything, and quacks were having a field day. In fact, the most that could be done was to keep the patient as comfortable as possible, let the fever run its course, and hope that the patient would recover.

The effects on daily living were many. Whole cities were struck by the flu and functioning with skeleton crews. In Philadelphia, for example, there was not much crime; almost no one was healthy enough to walk the streets.

Hospital wards all over the world were crowded, and there was a desperate shortage of doctors and nurses to care for the sick. From Great Britain to South Africa, public buildings were closed due to the dreaded influenza.

The disease which began in March of 1918 seemed to finally reach its peak in October. The mortality rate in New York City alone was approximately 800 people per day.

November 11, 1918 was the date of the signing of the Armistice to end World War I. Peace had come at last, and so had the end of the Spanish Flu epidemic. There is no logical explanation, though, as to why the flu disappeared.

Although little was known about the disease in 1918, scientists and doctors continued to research it. In the 1930s, the virus was identified and isolated; but, by then, the Spanish Flu was a thing of the past. Other strains of viruses have troubled modern man, but the record for death is still held by the Spanish Flu of 1918.

When a huge tank—58 feet high and over 90 feet wide—exploded and spewed its contents, the result was what Bostonians called and still call the "Great Molasses Flood."

It was indeed a sticky situation in Boston, when two million gallons of crude molasses exploded into a tidal wave of unbelievable force on Wednesday, January 15, 1919. The flood destroyed everything in its path.

The Purity Distillery Tank, a subsidiary of the United States Industrial Alcohol Company, was located at North End Park in a low-lying section of Commercial Street near Copps Hill. The tank itself stood 58 feet high and over 90 feet wide. It was said to be designed to hold 2,500,000 gallons of crude molasses, and, on that January day in 1919, it was filled to the top.

The weather on January 15 was 43°. Boston had warmed up con-siderably from a frigid low of 2° only three days before. People living in the old homes near the molasses tank were enjoying the warmer weather, as were the freight workers and the men in the pumping station. People all over the area, in fact, were enjoying the sunny, clear skies.

The aftermath of two million gallons of crude molasses exploding was devastation throughout the North End Park section in Boston.

At 12:30 p.m., though, a low, deep rumble was heard. This was quickly followed by the sound of ripping and tearing. Before people had time to even question what the noise was, a louder boom seemed to rock the earth and the huge molasses tank broke open. All of its black, sticky contents were released. The molasses roared free of its tank; moving like an angry river, it covered everything and everybody in its way.

The loading pit of the freight yard across the street was filled with five feet of molasses in a matter of minutes. Four loaded freight cars were tossed about on the tracks like toys, and a half-loaded car was hurled through the corrugated iron walls of the terminal. A two-ton iron plate was hurtled 200 feet from the force of the moving molasses.

People within range of the molasses did not live to tell about the flood. Six city workers, enjoying the day, had been eating their lunches outside; they died in moments. Others were trapped in the buildings where they worked and died as the molasses sucked them down. Still others died in their nearby homes. The lucky ones were those people who could climb to upper stories. One newspaper account of the flood stated that people were trapped upstairs for several days.

Fire Chief Peter McDonough received the first alarm at 12:40 p.m. The reports which came in caused him to send out another alarm for more rescue workers. Sailors from the nearby Charleston Navy Yard also came to offer help.

Walking was extremely difficult in the sticky, crude molasses which flooded the streets.

The force of the molasses hurled a freight car through the walls of the terminal building.

The awful wreckage called for the use of ladders so that firemen and others involved in the rescue could reach down to pull the dead and injured from the sticky, black debris. Bodies actually floated in the molasses river.

Fifteen bodies were recovered that day and six more were found later. Of the 40 people who were injured, all survived after being taken to nearby hospitals for treatment.

The day after the molasses had done its worst, the cleanup began. Firemen with heavy hoses tried to wash the molasses off the buildings and the collected debris. The sticky mess went up as high as two stories in many places. When this water hit the molasses, yellow suds billowed up which delayed the cleanup action. It was a long time before the gutters could carry off the sticky mess. The North End reeked of the molasses stench for weeks.

The actual cause of the explosion was never fully proved but over 100 lawsuits were filed against the United States Industrial Alcohol Company. It took six years of seemingly endless hearings before the legal action was completed. At that time, settlements of one million dollars were paid out by the company.

The courts decided that the owners of the molasses tank were responsible. The tank, although of huge proportions, was not strong enough to hold the amount of crude molasses which had been stored in it.

The "Great Molasses Flood," as it is sometimes called, was a black, sticky tidal wave of destruction. Today, the people who live and work in the North End area of Boston still remember that awful event of January 15, 1919.

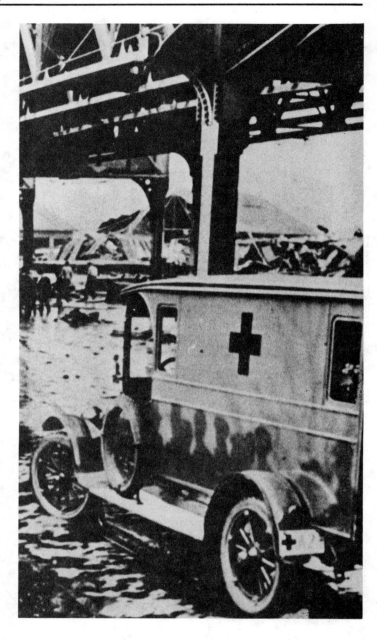

After the collapse of the molasses tank, the American Red Cross was on hand to help with the cleanup operation and provide food or shelter for those in need.

TOKYO AND YOKOHAMA DEVASTATED

Death Toll 150,000
100,000 Severely Injured
Homes Turned to Dust

The final death toll from the earthquake and ensuing fire at Tokyo and Yokohama was approximately 150,000; another 100,000 people were severely injured. This was the worst earthquake to hit Japan since 1856, and no one could accurately count the dead and homeless. Both cities were destroyed. Ultimately, though, both cities were rebuilt.

Saturday morning, shortly before noon, the citizens of Tokyo and Yokohama were preparing for lunch in their usual manner. The population of these two cities was over two million people. As three consecutive shocks struck both places, Tokyo and Yokohama crashed to the ground.

Almost every important building in Tokyo was destroyed by the earthquake. Shrines, temples, and churches were all reduced to rubble in an instant. The giant tower of the Asakusa temple killed some 700 people when it crashed. Hundreds of thousands of homes turned to dust, and people began to panic in their search for safety.

Tokyo and Yokohama were both levelled by the worst earthquake to hit Japan since 1856. This scene shows the devastation left in Yokohama.

The quake at Yokohama created much the same kind of debris and rubble as found in Tokyo. Water mains were broken and electrical wires were snapped. Since Yokohama was a port city, many of the buildings on the river embankment—including the American Hospital—slid right into the water. Destruction was everywhere.

As in the case of the earthquake at San Francisco in 1906, the quake alone was not responsible for the terrible loss of life. Fire broke out almost immediately in both cities and spread uncontrollably over a large area. Fire cyclones of intense heat formed and swept through the cities.

Forty thousand people huddled together in Tokyo at a clothing depot; they were instantly suffocated by a roaring cyclone of fire. In Yokohama, people raced to the canals, plunging themselves into the water only to have their heads and exposed body parts charred beyond recognition.

Irrationally, in Tokyo, some people blamed the effects of the earthquake and the fires on the Koreans. This led to rioting in the streets and the killing of anyone who even faintly resembled a Korean. Approximately 3,000 Koreans suffered because of the ignorance of others.

Conditions were so bad in Tokyo and Yokohama that martial law had to be declared. There was no water. There was no food. Dysentery and typhoid were to take even more lives before help could alleviate the terrible conditions in Japan.

At first, the world was confused by the reports of disaster. Since Tokyo was cut off completely, it was from

Yokohama that word went out about the earthquake and the fires. Nearby cargo ships hastened to the port of Yokohama bringing much-needed supplies. It took several days before Tokyo itself had communication lines with the outside world.

Appeals for aid were answered from as far away as Britain and the United States. Emergency supplies and medical teams were sent to the area as quickly as possible. Citizens of San Francisco, with the memories of their own earthquake just a few years behind them, were especially generous in their aid.

Since there was no water with which to fight the flames, people watched helplessly as their homes burned in front of their very eyes.

People were forced to wait on streetcar tracks in front of their crushed houses for help to arrive. The area shown here did not suffer from the fires which broke out and took almost as many lives as the actual quake.

Many thousands of people were killed by fire. Here, victims lay as they fell, while the living attempted to identify the dead.

EPILOGUE

The Japanese were then, as now, a sturdy, adaptable people. Within a comparatively short seven years, the cities of Tokyo and Yokohama were rebuilt. The massive shocks of the great earthquake of 1923 were only memories to those who had managed to survive.

ST. FRANCIS DAM—WHERE NONE SURVIVED

March 13, 1928

The St. Francis Dam had burst, and billions of gallons of water rushed through the Santa Clara Valley just after midnight on March 13. Few if any in the way of the water lived to tell about it.

After much controversy from the citizens of California, the St. Francis Dam was built and finished in May, 1926. The reason for building the dam was to provide water for the city of Los Angeles. The location of the dam was to be across the San Francisquito Canyon, some 15 miles above the town of Saugus. Here, vast quantities of water could be stored and then, if needed, moved rapidly to the city by aqueduct.

The people who lived in and around the canyon area did not want the water dammed there. The ranchers felt this was keeping badly-needed water from their own lands; fruit and vegetable growers in the Santa Clara Valley felt the same way. Although they protested the building of the dam as long as they could, they were not able to stop the construction.

Billions of gallons of water were released when the St. Francis Dam gave way. Only the center portion of the dam held.

This highway bridge was torn in half from the force of the water.

The dam had mammouth proportions. It reached 175 feet above the streambed it covered and was 175 feet thick at its base. The top of the dam measured 16 feet thick. It was considered to be of the highest engineering standards and worth every penny of the $1,300,000 it cost.

On March 12, a maintenance crew discovered trouble. Muddy water seemed to be seeping around or under the concrete base of the dam. The chief of the Los Angeles Bureau of Water and Power, William Mulholland, was summoned to the site at noon. His inspection showed that there was indeed a leak. Heavy rains which occurred days before the inspection might have contributed to the seepage, but Mulholland declared there was nothing to be done at that time.

Twelve hours later, the St. Francis Dam gave way. No one knows which side of the dam burst first, but, in a matter of minutes, both sides of the concrete structure had collapsed. Oddly enough, the center portion of the dam held.

Billions of gallons of water released by the broken dam roared down to the sea, carrying everything in its path.

Only the center section of the St. Francis Dam remained standing. The entire town of Santa Paula was buried under the raging water.

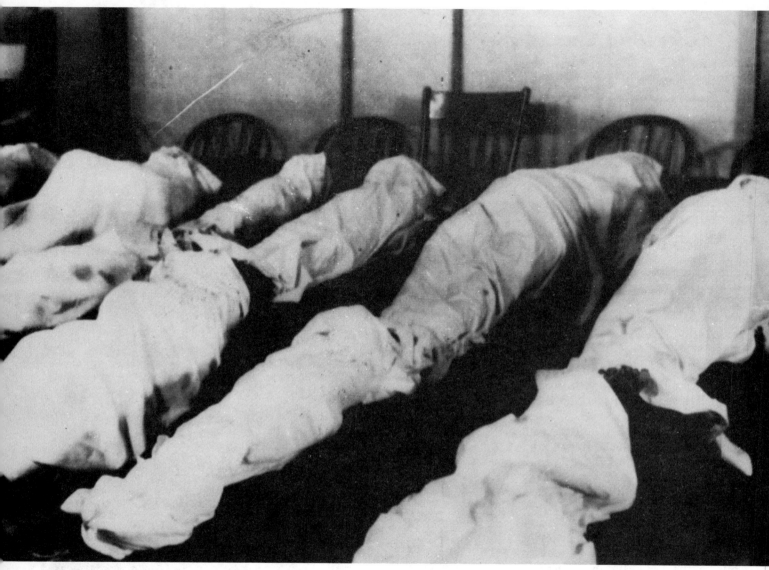

Over 450 people lost their lives. Here, rows of the dead await identification.

A bridge across the Santa Clara River was swept away by the water. Although it was the middle of the night, there were some automobiles on the highway at that time. They were also swept away and washed out to sea. No one knows, however, the exact number of cars that were out on that terrible night.

The town of Santa Paula, situated below the St. Francis Dam, had a population of approximately 450 people. The water destroyed all of the homes and killed all of the people who had resided there.

When the water subsided, a lengthy legal trial was held to establish blame for the disaster. Facts came to light which were astounding. The dam had actually been built on a fault—a weakness in the earth's crust which was subject to sudden shifts. Geologists would have recognized this as a dangerous place to build a dam, but the engineers did not.

Still another factor was the material on which the dam rested. It looked like solid rock—until a piece of that rock was dropped into water. What had been solid, then dissolved into a muddy mess.

The city of Los Angeles accepted the responsibility for what had happened and claims were paid to survivors for each relative killed. Thirty million dollars were paid out before all claims were satisfied—indeed a greater price than the dam itself had cost to build.

Many people have never heard of the collapse of the St. Francis Dam, but it did change the course of history as far as the building of dams went. As a result of the tragedy of St. Francis, not only engineers were hired to build future dams, but geologists as well. A strong structure was not all that was needed; it had to be built on a firm, natural foundation in order to safely satisfy the needs of all.

The British steamship, the *Vestris,* was traveling from New York to Buenos Aires with 128 passengers on board and a crew of 210. The ship belonged to the Lamport and Holt Line and was also carrying a heavy load of freight. Later opinions declared that the overload of freight was, among other things, responsible for the sinking of the ship.

It was November 12, and the *Vestris* was 240 miles out of port when she encountered heavy weather. Captain William Carey had already been told that the *Vestris* was shipping water through an ash-ejector and a coal-chute door. The shipping of water was causing a list to the starboard which even the passengers were aware of. There was difficulty in keeping afoot in the cabins because of the ship's angle.

Captain Carey sent out a CQ call (a British maritime stand-by call) at 8:37 a.m. By 10:00 a.m., the *Vestris* was still in trouble with a very sharp list to the starboard. The captain ordered an SOS.

Heavy weather caused the British ship Vestris to sink 240 miles from port. The death toll was 110 people.

The progression of radio calls which came from the *Vestris* best describes conditions on the ship. At 10:45 a.m., the distress call said "Rush at all speed." At 11:03 a.m., the cry was "Oh, please come at once."

"Ship sinking slowly" went across the air at 11:07 a.m. At 1:17 p.m., the message was "Can't wait any longer. Going to abandon." The last message from the sinking *Vestris*, which went out at 1:25 p.m., said "We are taking to the lifeboats."

In the case of the *Vestris*, unlike the ill-fated *Titanic* of former times, there were enough lifeboats on board to hold twice the number of people. But the first rescue ships on the scene found no trace of either the *Vestris* or the lifeboats.

Unlike the sinking of the Titanic, the Vestris had sufficient lifeboats for the number of people on board. Shown here is a full lifeboat of survivors.

The first rescue ship to arrive was the American Shipper. It had seen the first lifeboat of the Vestris drifting in the sea.

It was not until 4:00 a.m. on the morning of November 13 that the S.S. *American Shipper* picked up a lifeboat. Still later, seven more lifeboats were found and rescued. The survivors were returned to New York. However, 110 people did not return.

Bitter recriminations were hurled at the captain of the *Vestris* when the survivors made port. More than 3/4 of the crew had survived and less than half of the passengers. Of the 49 women and children on the *Vestris,* only eight women were saved.

The charge of negligence was raised by an angry press. The British blamed American agents in New York for allowing the *Vestris* to sail overloaded. Other charges were leveled at Captain Carey for not sending out the SOS earlier in the day. Still others proclaimed that the *Vestris* was not seaworthy in the first place.

Even the lowering of the lifeboats was criticized. Those on the port side of the *Vestris* were loaded with women and children. Captain Carey held off the lowering of those boats until it was too late. When the boats were finally lowered, they capsized into the sea because of the terrible listing of the *Vestris.* Some said that the captain held off in hopes that rescue ships would arrive before it was necessary to put the lifeboats in the water. If this was so, it was a vain hope.

The British Board of Trade conducted an investigation into the sinking of the *Vestris.* Since the *Vestris* was a British ship with a British captain, the Board was kinder than the newspapers had been. They blamed American agents for allowing the *Vestris* to sail overloaded. They declared that Captain Carey was too optimistic in his hopes for rescue—a mild chastisement for the captain's poor judgement. The lowering of the lifeboats was called "imprudent."

Like most investigations, this one by the British Board of Inquiry could not change what had happened. The *Vestris* was gone and so was Captain Carey. The captain had gone down with his ship—and the report which came back said that, as he walked down the side of the *Vestris* into the water, his last words were:

"My God, I am not to blame for this."

These survivors of the Vestris arrived in New York aboard the Berlin two days after the Vestris sank.

The burnt and charred framework was all that remained of the R101, Britain's airship which claimed to be the largest in the world. The airship crashed in the vicinity of Beauvais, France.

Britain's Air Minister, Lord Thompson, was determined that the *R101*, a luxuriously-appointed airship, should make her maiden voyage to India by way of Egypt. The *R101* was to be Britain's claim to long-distance travel.

The *R100*, a privately-funded airship, had already flown to Canada and back successfully. Lord Thompson's answer to this success was to announce that the *R101* would depart for India on October 4. Whether the *R101* was actually ready for the long

flight was open to dispute later on. But Lord Thompson was determined that Britain's airship was going to leave—with himself on board.

Prior to its embarkation, the *R101* had undergone some rather severe structural alterations. The ship had actually been cut in half to insert an extra bay and then put back together again. There had been no test flight after these alterations were done.

Of the 54 people on board, only seven were lucky enough to escape. Here, bodies of the victims are being transported from the wreckage.

Although the R101 burst into flames after it exploded, the British flag was only partially burned.

The fittings of the airship were luxurious—an attempt to equal the splendor of the ocean liners. Indeed, the inside of the rooms had marvelous appointments. There was silver cutlery, potted palms, and heavy Axminster carpeting throughout. There were gold and white staterooms and even a fireproof smoking lounge. Travel in the *R101* was to be an exciting affair.

On the evening of October 4, the *R101* was moored at Cardington, just north of London. Fifty-four people prepared for takeoff, including six passengers. Among these passengers were Sir Sefton Brancker, Director of Civil Aviation at the Ministry, and Lord Thompson.

In this day and age of weighing baggage before boarding an airplane, it is amazing that no effort was made to total what weight was aboard the *R101*. Lord Thompson's effects alone were reported to weigh as much as 24 people. Whether this was a later exaggeration of the truth will never be known.

The airship left Cardington at 6:36 p.m. Those on board were relaxed and preparing to enjoy a long, comfortable flight. Some of those watching the takeoff later recalled that the ship had dipped sharply and had been forced to drop a great deal of water ballast to gain height.

Shortly before 2 a.m., the ship had crossed the Channel and was flying over France. Routine wireless messages were being sent back to London that all was well and the passengers were preparing for bed.

After 2:07 a.m., there were no more messages from the *R101*. Almost a minute later, people in the vicinity of Beauvais were awakened by a loud noise and streaks of light soaring across the sky. The *R101* had gone down, exploded, and burst into sheets of flame.

Of the 54 people on board, only seven were lucky enough to escape. Six of the survivors were in the engine car at the time of the explosion. This was what saved their lives, as a bursting water ballast tank covered them with water and gave them enough time to jump from the burning ship. The seventh survivor managed to hack a hole in the *R101* and jump through to safety. All seven were taken to a nearby hospital and treated for burns.

Lord Thompson, who had been so certain that the *R101* would bring glory to Britain, died in the explosion.

This was to be the end of Britain's attempts at launching the large, lighter-than-air airships. It was to be yet another step toward the end of the great dirigibles which were then rulers of the sky.

The dead were brought back to England for burial in a common grave at Cardington, very close to the spot where they took off for their journey.

Final blame for the failure of the *R101* was placed on public policy. Had there not been pressure on Lord Thompson for that October 4 takeoff to India, it is possible that corrections of the great ship might have been made and the whole history of the airship gone in another direction.

As to the cause of the disaster, no one could be exactly sure what had happened. Was the ship carrying too much weight? Or did the great structure of the *R101* actually split apart? Did the minute holes in the gas bags which the *R101* carried cause its destruction? We will never know.

Experts, who flew to the scene after the crash of the airship, stated that the structure of the R101 had actually split apart. The twisted, burned-out remains of the airship were to be the end of Britain's attempts to fly lighter-than-air airships.

FLOOD WATERS OF THE MIGHTY YANGTSE RIVER

August, 1931

83

Summer in the Yangtse becomes a raging torent

The Chinese are a patient people accustomed to the will of heaven. They've lived through flood, drought, famine, and civil war. When their homes were destroyed, they rebuilt. When their crops failed, they planted again.

One thing which is constant in China is the mighty Yangtse River. This river—originating in Tibet and ending in the Yangtse Valley—is 3,200 miles long. It is the third largest river in the world and carries silt and top soil in its water which enrich the banks alongside. This silt and topsoil are also responsible for the water's muddy color.

The raging waters of the Yangtse River brought death by flood, starvation, and exposure in the terrible days of 1931. This scene in Hankow shows how the streets of the city turned into rivers.

When the Yangtse flows along peacefully, heavy junks move slowly and gracefully through its waters. Even steamships travel between Shanghai and Hankow, carrying produce and goods to the cities for trade.

The Grand Canal, with its many dikes, runs along part of the Yangtse. At certain points on the top of the dikes, narrow towns have been built. In some places, the dike is 15 to 20 feet higher than the plain below.

Although Hankow suffered from the flooding, the business of the city was carried on by wading through the waters or paddling in boats through the deeper areas.

At this stretch of the Grand Canal, the dikes held fast. Note the long, narrow town which was built right along the top of the dike.

Nearly four weeks after the first breaks of the Grand Canal in August, torrents of water still poured into the plains below.

The summer of 1931 was a wet one in China. Rains throughout the month of August had swollen the Yangtse River. By the end of the month, the once-gentle Yangtse was a raging torrent, causing death and destruction as it made its way through China to the sea beyond.

The New York Times headline of August 30, 1931 captured the essence of the story:

Patient China is Scourged Once More

But what that headline does not describe is the devastation which occurred. Streets in the towns of Hankow, Wuchang, and Hanyang were obliterated by the muddy waters. In fact, the people in Hankow used their boats to get from one end of town to the other.

In some places, the waters of the Yangtse broke down the dikes of the Grand Canal, pouring nearly four weeks worth of accumulated rain onto the plains below. Where the dikes held fast, the waters rose to many feet above their normal level.

Figures vary as to the number of people who were lost in this dreadful flood. They range from 140,000 dead to as many as 250,000. Some estimates state that over two million people were left homeless due to the angry waters.

After the flood waters calmed, those who survived went on to rebuild homes out of the muddy aftermath. Rice fields were again planted and the Chinese continued to live on the banks of the Yangtse River.

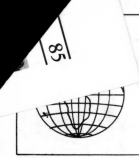
DIRIGIBLE AKRON CRASH AT SEA

April 4, 1933

"DIRIGIBLE AKRON CRASHES IN LIGHTNING STORM AT SEA . . ." This was the headline which spilled across the front page of the New York Times on Tuesday, April 4, 1933. However, this was not the first headline to have been written about the American airship, U.S.S. *Akron*, at that time.

The *Akron* was built for the Navy by the Goodyear Zeppelin Corporation and christened by Mrs. Herbert Hoover in August, 1931. The ship measured 785 feet in length and carried over 6,750,000 cubic feet of helium. It was the largest airship in the world. Indeed, this giant lighter-than-air ship was considered by some to be unwieldy.

While the *Akron* was still under construction, there was an attempt at sabotage—reportedly by a communist agent. The ship's troubles, though, were just beginning. At completion, it was discovered that the airship was ten percent heavier than the original specifications. Despite this, however, the *Akron* took to the air as a Navy dirigible.

A misunderstood order may have been the reason that the U.S.S. Akron crashed into the sea and killed all but three of the men on board. Here, a section of the wreckage is shown being hauled from the ocean.

There was an accident on the ground at Lakehurst, New Jersey, in 1932. The *Akron* suffered much damage and had to be repaired before further flights could take place.

Later in 1932, still another mishap befell the *Akron*. It was completing a transcontinental trip and preparing to land near San Diego. A crowd of 10,000 spectators stood waiting to see the great ship land. Suddenly, the *Akron* was hoisted back into the air by an upward current. Three members of the landing crew were hauled up with the *Akron* on the end of the mooring lines. Only one of those men was able to pull himself into the ship; the other two died.

The press roared its disapproval of the *Akron* and considered it to be jinxed. Rear Admiral William A. Moffet, the father of the American Airship Program, did not agree. He was quoted as saying:

''To my knowledge she is the best airship that has ever been built.''

Rear Admiral Moffet was on board the *Akron* on April 4. The ship's commander was Captain Frank Carey McCord and the executive commander was Lieutenant Commander Herbert V. Wiley.

At 12:30 a.m. on the fateful day, the *Akron* was about 25 miles off Barnegat, New Jersey, and cruising at an altitude of 1,600 feet. There were 76 men on board. Suddenly, air currents hurdled the ship about as if it were a football. The *Akron* dropped to 700 feet before it plummeted into the sea. Within a few minutes, the ship was pounded to pieces by the heavy waves.

Rescue ships searching the area were only able to locate three of the men who had been on board; the rest were swallowed up by the ocean. Among those who survived was Lieutenant Commander Wiley. He was later to testify with some shocking facts before the Board of Inquiry.

A misunderstood order from Captain McCord may have been the reason that the *Akron* went down. Com-

The U.S.S. Falcon operated the salvage apparatus which recovered the control cabin—shown here being raised from the deep.

Naval officers examined the remains of the Akron. The crash of this airship was another example of how unstable these lighter-than-air airships were and made them a thing of the past for American aviation.

mander Wiley said that the captain had ordered a shift of 15° in course. This order, though, was misunderstood and the course was shifted 50°. It was this mistake which sent the *Akron* to its doom. Captain McCord, however, did not live to answer any of the charges which were levelled against him.

Two more deaths were attributed to the *Akron*. A small rescue blimp, known as the *J3*, was sent out to aid in the search for survivors. The *J3* could not handle the strong winds and also crashed into the sea, killing two of her crew. The total number of dead was now 75.

Although much of the ill-fated *Akron* was eventually salvaged, the results of examination only showed that the ship had broken up when she made contact with the sea. Those people in favor of constructing more dirigibles in

this country felt this was a good reason to continue. According to them, the dirigible was airworthy.

However, the loss of the *Akron* was to be the beginning of the end for American dirigibles. Only the sister-ship, the *Macon*, was still operable. But, two years later, the *Macon* also went down at sea. Two members of its crew died.

Chairman Vinson, of the House Naval Affairs Committee, made the final announcement of the fate of dirigibles in the United States: ''You can take it from me, there won't be any more big airships built.''

The lighter-than-air airship was a thing of the past in American aviation.

The *Morro Castle*, the last word in luxury liners, was heading to New York City after a cruise to Havana. Her captain, Robert Wilmotte, took great pride in this vessel.

Built in 1930 at a cost of $5 million, the *Morro Castle* offered her passengers the finest in dance floors, dining rooms, and staterooms—not to mention providing writing rooms and libraries. She was said to have all the latest equipment, including fire equipment and two radio sets. The lifeboats aboard could hold 470 more people than were actually on board.

On the afternoon of September 8, Captain Wilmotte was preparing to bathe when a sharp pain gripped him.

Panic Begins

The cause of death was officially listed as a heart attack. The 231 crew members and the 318 passengers were duly notified, and First Officer William Warms assumed command. As this was the final night of the cruise, none of the parties going on were cancelled despite the captain's death.

This undated picture of the Morro Castle shows the luxury liner afloat with all flags flying. Her last trip was from Havana to New York City.

Smoke was first noticed around midnight. People were aware of the smell, but no one paid any attention. Later, a female passenger wandered into a writing room and found the ceiling ablaze. A crewman noticed smoke and sparks coming from a stokehole. Precious minutes ticked by as the crew tried vainly to put out the blaze.

The fire spread rapidly through every air shaft, porthole, and ventilator. The elevators and stairways were

The lifeboats shown here were unapproachable during the height of the fire. The death toll was 134.

soon consumed. The electrical system was burned out and the telephone network was destroyed. Official calls of danger came shortly before 3 a.m., and the crew alerted the sleeping passengers by banging on anything they could find.

Because the ship was only 30 minutes from shore, the captain did not think it necessary to abandon ship or send out an SOS. However, some of the passengers panicked and jumped from the ship; they were drowned.

By 3:30 a.m., the ship's steering equipment stopped functioning and it listed helplessly in the Atlantic Ocean. Flames were leaping all around her and hysteria prevailed.

Many life jackets burned in the staterooms, while frightened passengers fought over those few still untouched on the decks. The crew abandoned their passengers in an effort to save their own lives. They ripped off all *Morro Castle* identification from their uniforms in a desperate effort to escape the ship and their own decision-making responsibilities.

When fire was first sighted on the Morro Castle, the great ship was only one half hour from shore. The acting captain did not think it necessary to abandon ship or send out an SOS. This picture shows the burned-out ship arriving at Asbury Park, New Jersey.

The naval investigation which followed the fire showed that six of the ship's 12 lifeboats were still tied to it. Here is one of the lifeboats which was lowered approaching the rescue ship, the Monarch of Bermuda.

Six life rafts were lowered, each with a holding capacity of 40 people or more. The first raft contained seven crewmen and three passengers. Another contained 31 people—two passengers and 29 crewmen.

Unable to find an available life raft or too frightened to wait, whole families were jumping ship together. A newly-married couple jumped and clung to life for several hours in the sea—holding on to a bloated corpse. The bridegroom was drowned when a wave washed him under. A mother pushed her young child into the sea; he drowned before she could jump in after him.

A rescue effort of major proportions was initiated by the Coast Guard after the only SOS that the *Morro Castle* sent was received. The rescue boats plucked a total of

The Morro Castle beached itself at Asbury Park, New Jersey—a smouldering hulk of what had once been a great luxury liner.

224 people from the ocean. Lifeboats from the ill-fated liner saved only 85. A few people were able to swim ashore through the warm Atlantic waters.

Of the 318 passengers on board, 90 died; of the 231 crew members, only 44 were lost.

A naval investigation began immediately. While the cause of the fire was never determined, the findings from the investigation were very disturbing. Only seven crew-men were on duty when the fire broke out. No crew member knew where the heavy fire doors were located which might have kept the fire isolated.

The ship's crew and passengers had never had a fire drill. In fact, six of the ship's 12 lifeboats were still tied to the ship where they burned—and all of the lifeboats were in poor condition.

Perhaps the most startling fact was the crew's poor re-sponse to the danger. Of the first 98 people to leave the

Thousands of visitors flocked to Asbury Beach to survey the skeleton of the Morro Castle.

burning ship, 92 were crew members. The man responsi-ble for hiring these men could neither read nor write. He was only concerned with hiring cheap labor.

Human error, not the fire, brought a tragic and blazing end to this luxury liner. Poor judgment and panic caused

134 people to lose their lives on that September night. The *Morro Castle* itself was a burned out shell. The sur-vivors would live with the smell of smoke, the roar of fire and the cries for help for the rest of their lives.

"WET" GAS CAUSES SCHOOL EXPLOSION

The Consolidated School at New London, Texas, looked like this before the horrible blast virtually demolished the building.

The Consolidated School at New London, Texas, was set in the middle of thousands of oil derricks. The school was built with funds from the oil industry which surrounded it and was one of the most up-to-date rural schools in the country.

The school had everything from home economic kitchens to modern playground equipment. In the 1930s, with the days of depression still fresh in the minds of most people, the Consolidated School was indeed very special. It had been built at a cost of over a million dollars. Texas oil money had razed a small wooden schoolhouse to erect the modern school complex.

It was 3:05 p.m. on March 18, when a terrible explosion was heard for miles around. An oft-quoted description of the blast came from the school superintendent, William C. Shaw, who happened to be out of the main building at the time:

"The roof just lifted up. Then the walls fell out and the roof fell in."

This aerial photograph shows the ridge of earth which marked the foundation of the Consolidated School after the explosion occurred. The number of students and teachers killed in this disaster was 297.

Rescue workers from nearby oil fields and hysterical parents rushed to the scene. There, they began to dig into the debris in hopes of finding the children alive.

A series of smaller blasts followed the first one in quick succession, but these were hardly noticed in the confusion which followed. Debris and bodies were all around.

The original casualty toll was estimated at 455 people. The figure would have been much higher if the explosion had occurred earlier. As it was, the primary school had already been dismissed. At 3:05 p.m., there were 690 high-school students in the building and more than 40 teachers.

Men from the nearby oil fields rushed to the scene. Hysterical parents began digging into the debris looking for any sign of life. They had to be forcibly stopped so that rescue work could be done more carefully.

Within an hour, things were organized, and the men removed bodies and bricks one by one. The gory work continued on into the night, and the bodies which were removed were taken to improvised morgues or nearby hospitals. Four-hundred-and-thirty-seven people survived the explosion, although many suffered serious injuries.

Some bodies were so severely burned that identification was almost impossible. Fingerprints of the dead were sent to Dallas for positive identification. Most of the high-school students had gone on a field trip to the Texas Centennial Exposition the year before and had been finger-

This section of wall in the Consolidated School did not fall in the explosion, but debris was piled high all around.

printed. This now aided in the identification of those who were mutilated beyond recognition.

What was the cause of the explosion? Superintendent Shaw, in mourning for his own son who was killed in the explosion, explained that the school was trying to economize their heating bills by using ''wet'' gas—a waste product which is a mixture of several different components and actually costs nothing. In order to avail themselves of the ''wet'' gas, the school janitor had installed a connection to the pipes containing the waste product. This was a common but dangerous practice in Texas at that time—the danger being that the heating capacity and ignition point of the ''wet'' gas were not constant. What heated well one day might very well explode the next. However, no one will even know what spark touched off the explosion.

The savings of $250 to $350 in monthly heating bills did not make up for the loss of life. The official death toll was 297. There was a mass funeral on the Sunday following the explosion.

Children are seen here mourning some of their classmates. The town of New London was justifiably saddened at the loss of life which occurred in the unnecessary explosion of the Consolidated School.

EPILOGUE

As to future use of waste or ''wet'' gas, the lawmakers of oil-producing states quickly passed legislation to insure that a tragedy such as this could not happen again. Oil companies are now compelled by law to burn the waste or ''wet'' gas at its source; no one is to use it for heating purposes.

The parents of those who died in the explosion of the Consolidated School might justifiably feel that, for them, too little was done too late. Nothing could bring back the children and teachers who lost their lives unnecessarily at New London in 1937.

FLAMES FROM THE SKY AT LAKEHURST

May 6, 1937

The airship *Hindenburg's* maiden flight of the 1937 season was due to end at the Lakehurst Naval Air Station in New Jersey. Since this was a routine landing, the crowds that gathered under the clear skies to await the arrival of the 804-foot dirigible consisted of families meeting passengers. However, as the *Hindenburg* was touted as the world's greatest air luxury liner, some members of the press were also on hand to cover the event for radio and the newspapers.

The *Hindenburg* was the largest airship ever constructed and the pride of Germany's Adolph Hitler. The ship was commissioned in 1936 and was the 118th zeppelin-type airship built by Germany. It was powered by four diesel engines and its lifting power came from highly-flammable hydrogen gas.

Only the wealthy could afford to book passage on the *Hindenburg,* as the cost was $400 for a one-way ticket. But, for those who had the means, it was an exciting way to travel. The ship's 25 staterooms were luxuriously appointed and there was a passengers' dining room and prome-

nade as well as a lounge with a grand piano. There was even a large ballroom. The *Hindenburg* was indeed the last word in elegant travel accommodations.

German's luxury airship, the Hindenburg, exploded into flames at the Lakehurst Naval Air Station in New Jersey. A horrified world listened intently to the radio announcement by Herbert Morrison—"It's broken into flames. . ."

Captain Max Pruss was piloting the *Hindenburg,* and his crew of 61 helped to make the 36 passengers who were on board comfortable during the 76 hours it took to cross the Atlantic. New York and the journey's end were in sight, and the early May evening was still bright with sunlight.

At approximately 7 p.m., the *Hindenburg* made a perfect approach to the Lakehurst Naval Air Station. Moor-

Only a skeleton of the zeppelin remained after the fire. The ship had been preparing to dock at the Naval Air Station after its successful trip across the ocean.

ing lines were thrown to the waiting crews below. Herbert Morrison, a radio announcer with Station WLS, Chicago, was relaxed in his description of the approaching airship.

Suddenly, everything changed. The tail section of the *Hindenburg,* which bore the German swastika, burst into flames. The time was 7:23 p.m. Herbert Morrison now told quite a different story to a listening world!

"It's broken into flames . . . Oh this is terrible . . . it is burning, bursting into flames and is falling . . . This is one of the worst catastrophies in the world . . . Oh! It's a terrific sight . . . Oh the humanity . . ."

The ship was only 75 feet above the ground when the fire broke out. Those standing below could see the people who were on board. The tail of the airship began to sink to the ground, and, in a matter of seconds, the fire spread to the rest of the ship.

Miraculously, some people did survive by jumping from the *Hindenburg's* flaming belly to the ground below. The last to jump was Captain Pruss. He eventually returned to Germany, still convinced of the value of this type of airship.

The *Hindenburg* explosion took 36 lives in all; 22 crew members, 13 passengers and 1 ground crew member who could not run clear of the falling ship. Although the actual cause of the explosion was never proved, this marked not only the end of the *Hindenburg,* but the end of the zeppelin era.

The Hindenburg was only 75 feet above the ground when the explosion and fire occurred. The disaster claimed a total of 36 lives. The ground crew can be seen in this picture.

HURRICANE SWEEPS NEW ENGLAND

Flood-Control Ignored

In September of 1938, the news was filled with disturbing accounts of increasing tensions in Europe. Names such as Hitler, Chamberlain, and the Sudetenland were becoming familiar to all Americans. Perhaps it was due to the severity of growing problems in Europe that few people paid attention to the weather reports in the United States.

On September 18, a storm was traveling northwest of Puerto Rico, 900 miles southeast of Miami. Weather bulletins advised the Miami area to prepare for a hurricane.

Disaster Strikes

By the 19th, it became apparent that the storm would miss Florida. It had changed course and was traveling parallel to the state in a northerly direction. By now, its diameter was 240 miles and it was moving at 15 miles per hour.

The fury of the flood waters is shown here at Providence, Rhode Island, during the hurricane which swept through New England. This scene of floating dock houses and a broken railroad bridge are typical of the damage which occurred throughout the hurricane area.

Then the storm started to pick up speed; it was traveling at 50 miles per hour, three times faster than any previous hurricane. In 12 hours, the storm traveled 600 miles; it became clear that the North Atlantic states—from New Jersey to Vermont—were facing a storm of disastrous proportions.

It had been raining for several days when the hurricane slammed into New England with terrific force. New Yorkers saw billboards topple to the streets under the storm's pressure. Electricity and telephone and radio services were disrupted. The 120 mile-an-hour winds were strong enough to sway the Empire State Building four inches. Trolley wires were blown down and trains couldn't run over flooded tracks.

By September 22, New York was brought to its knees. The hurricane had virtually paralyzed the city. Long Island was hit by a tidal wave, washing away many expensive summer homes.

One home, with its owners clinging to the roof in order to escape the rising flood, was rocked from its foundations. Vengeful waters washed the house across Moriches Bay and deposited it and its startled inhabitants on the Westhampton Golf Course.

Connecticut reported several highways closed—flooded with 8½ inches of water from four days of rain. The storm raged on.

An express train in New Haven was blocked by the water and its 300 commuters were held prisoner by the flood. There was even some concern over the fate of actor James Cagney. The actor was relaxing in his home on Martha's Vineyard (off of Cape Cod) when the storm hit. Communication with Cagney was impossible.

By September 24, the storm had already taken the lives of 400 people. However, the hurricane was still not satisfied. Two hundred people were on the beaches at Watch Hill in Rhode Island watching the storm pound the shore.

The flood waters from the hurricane rose to six feet in the streets of Providence. The first floor in many buildings were flooded out, and automobiles were swept away by the force of the waters.

Rivers broke through strong dams, and flooding was prevalent throughout New England. Here, the waters of the Quinebaug River raced through a break in the Dyer Dam in Connecticut.

They were tragically washed out to sea by the mammouth waves. With this additional loss of life, it seemed as if Mother Nature was finished venting her anger.

The hurricane of 1938 killed more than 600 people up and down the New England coast. A thousand boats were lost or badly damaged; 57,000 homes were ruined beyond repair; 60,000 people were left homeless; and entire forests were levelled to the ground. The storm caused $1 billion worth of damage.

Food and medical supplies were rushed to the area and had to be air dropped to many towns. The National Guard patrolled the streets in some states to prevent looting and maintain law and order.

Angry charges were levelled at the Roosevelt administration for failing to enact a flood-control system for New England. Legislation such as this could have averted much of the damage.

A relief program, sponsored by the government, helped families begin to rebuild their homes and their lives, but once again, nature had proved her prowess over man.

These three burned out archways were located in front of the main entrance to the Cocoanut Grove nightclub. The club's name can still be seen above the arches.

The country was at war and Boston was filled with soldiers and sailors enjoying a last fling before going off to join the fighting in Europe. A major football game which had been played between Holy Cross and Boston had also attracted hoardes of out-of-towners to the city. The mood then was one of excitement as people delighted in the festivities.

The Cocoanut Grove was a comparatively new nightclub in Boston—only fifteen years old—and an exciting place to be. The club had two levels: a restaurant level above, where the floor show was held on a revolving stage, and the Melody Lounge below. The Melody Lounge had simulated leather on the walls, artificial palm trees standing tall between the tables and brightly-colored silk hangings on the ceiling.

Safety Violations Cited

Although the club's maximum capacity was 460, the club owner did not care that he was violating fire regulations by accomodating 800 to 1,000 people—and neither did his patrons on that fateful Saturday night.

At 10 p.m., bandleader Mickey Alpert was playing the "Star Spangled Banner" to announce the start of the floor show upstairs.

Cause Eludes Investigators

In the Melody Lounge, a customer wishing for more intimacy by his table removed a ceiling light bulb from its socket. The bartender sent over a young waiter—Stephen Tomaszewski—to replace the bulb. Stephen was employed illegally by the club as he was underage for night work. As he climbed on a chair in the dark corner, he innocently lit a match to see. Suddenly, one of the decorative palm trees caught fire, and, in a matter of seconds, the Cocoanut Grove became a flaming inferno.

This exterior view of the Cocoanut Grove shows the clouds of smoke which billowed out from the burning club. The death toll was 433.

Firemen hold up a woman who is being given the last rites of the Catholic Church during the awful night at the Cocoanut Grove.

Charred remains of chairs, ladies' slippers, and sheet music were all that was left after patrons rushed to avoid the enveloping flames.

No one will ever know whether it was the match that Stephen Tomaszewski lit which started the fire or a short circuit. (Stephen survived the night's disaster and later said he had blown out the match.) But whatever the cause, the results were horrible.

It was panic, though, not a lack of exits that caused such a great loss of life. There were, in all, nine exits leading from the Cocoanut Grove out onto the street: Four exit doors led to Piedmont Street, four more led to Shawmut Avenue and the big revolving door at the front of the club faced Broadway.

MANY DIE IN REVOLVING DOOR

Unfortunately, it was to the revolving door that people surged en masse. Since there was no way for the crowd to pass through, people pushed and shoved and walked on

This is what was left of the club's revolving door. Panicked people pushed, shoved, and walked on top of fallen bodies in an effort to reach this door and escape the flames behind them.

top of fallen bodies. When the firemen were able to get into the Broadway entrance, a grizzly sight met their eyes. Bodies were piled six feet deep behind the revolving door.

In the panic, people were stampeded. Some were impaled on broken glass from the narrow windows, while others actually died half in and half out of the building. Many died of asphyxiation caused by the black smoke which came from the club's imitation leather walls.

The firemen arrived on the scene fifteen minutes after the fire started and it took them only an hour to get the blaze under control. However, in those 60 minutes, 433 people died, yet still another 59 died in the hospitals. Thus, the total death count was a gruesome 492.

Rescue work went on all through the night. Local hospitals were constantly admitting casualties. Dead bodies lined hospital corridors, too badly burned to be immediately identified. Civil defense workers and the Red Cross were called in to help. Blood plasma was taken from the wartime blood banks and anti-burn drugs came from as far away as New York. Ultimately, martial law had to be declared in order to proceed with the cleanup operation.

EPILOGUE

Boston and the country were shocked at the results of the Cocoanut Grove fire. An inquiry was held the next day, but the actual cause of the fire could not be determined. Was the lighted match of Stephen Tomaszewski the primary cause of the blaze or was it a short circuit in the club's faulty electrical wiring? The Fire Commissioner could not prove either theory.

The Cocoanut Grove nightclub was never rebuilt; in fact, the ground on which it stood is now a parking lot. But the memory of the disaster of November 28, 1942 will still haunt our lives.

THE BURNING OF THE BIG TOP

The Ringling Brothers and Barnum and Bailey Circus held its first performance at Hartford, Connecticut, on July 5, 1944. Although the country was in the throes of war at this time, the circus was considered a necessary relief for the people on the home front. In fact, the circus had managed to keep close to its pre-war schedule.

Since the first performance received such good notices in the Hartford newspapers, many people planned to come see the only matinee on July 6.

The morning of the 6th was a typical summer day—with bright sunlight and high temperatures. By noon, the thermometer had already reached 90°. Performers were having trouble with their makeup, and the animal caretakers were trying to keep their wild charges as cool as possible.

The big top, as the main tent has always been called, was big indeed. It measured over 500 feet long, 250 feet wide, and 75 feet high. Although the tent could hold 12,000 people, there were only about half that number waiting to see the exciting circus acts.

The big top of the Ringling Brothers and Barnum and Bailey Circus measured over 500 feet in length, 250 feet in width, and 75 feet in height before it burned to ashes during the July matinee performance.

Flames and thick, black smoke made it difficult for the crowd to get out from under the big top. The number of people who burned to death in that fire was 168.

Prior to the Hartford performances, the tent had been waterproofed with a mixture of paraffin and gasoline. This waterproofing was intended to prolong the life of the canvas. But what it actually did was create a firetrap.

The circus began with its usual grand parade of animals. Merle Evans was conducting the band and performers in nearby dressing rooms were listening for their entrance cues.

The big cats—lions, tigers, and panthers—were just finishing their act at 2:30 p.m. As the animals were being led from the ring, all eyes in the stands focused on the famous "Flying Wallendas" balanced on the high wire. Looking down from that great height, Herman Wallenda saw a small tongue of flame licking at the canvas of the tent. Although those below did not know what he had seen, they saw him hurry the other Wallendas to their platforms and prepare to descend.

At the same moment, others saw the darting flames creeping up the side walls of the tent; however, most of the spectators were still unaware. Merle Evans instructed his band to play "The Stars and Stripes Forever"—the traditional disaster signal for circus people.

In his dressing room, "sad clown" Emmett Kelley heard the music, and so did his friend, another well-known clown, Felix Adler.

The fire made itself known to everyone all too quickly. In a matter of minutes, the big top was filled with smoke from the burning paraffin; flames were everywhere. Although the circus performers tried to calm the crowd, the air was soon filled with the panic-stricken cries of those who had come to the circus that day. People pushed and shoved to the nearest exits, walking on top of those who fell.

Emmett Kelley and Felix Adler both worked tirelessly to help people escape from the inferno. Midgets ran under the tent flaps showing frightened people ways to escape. There were some miraculous victories over the fire and some very brave deeds done. There were also many who could not be saved at all.

The canvas of the big top burned away all too rapidly. The center poles which held it up burned as well, crashing to the ground and pinning bodies under them. Thick smoke made it difficult to see, and panic made it increasingly hard to move about.

One-hundred-and-sixty-eight people burned to death at Hartford that day. Still another 250 were rushed to hospitals for treatment. The big top burned completely in only 15 minutes. This was considered one of the worst circus fires of all time. Emmett Kelley later described it as ''the longest afternoon of my life.''

The big top burned completely in 15 minutes, leaving behind the charred seats shown here.

The aftermath of the terrible fire shows collapsed animal rings and charred poles and bleacher seats.

This ruined ring of the circus was photographed after the fire burned itself out. The cause of the fire was never proved, but death claims against the circus' owners remained in the courts for 10 years.

EPILOGUE

The immediate cause of the Hartford circus fire was never proved. Did a careless cigarette start a pile of trash burning too near the tent or was it arson?

Responsibility for the fire was laid at the doors of the circus' top brass. Hartford courts charged five circus officials with involuntary manslaughter. Death claims for fire victims remained in the courts for ten years before they were all settled.

However, those who lived through that fiery day, will never forget the cries of fear when the big top burned to the ground.

GAS TANKS EXPLODE AT EAST SIDE GAS CO.

The gas explosion which occurred on October 20, 1944 affected residents within 50 blocks of Cleveland's East Side. After the initial explosion of the tanks which contained liquified natural gas, havoc was created by the ensuing fires, lack of utilities, and danger of further explosion.

The East Side Gas Company had built their tanks in Cleveland in 1940 with the purpose of storing liquified natural gas. Three of the huge tanks were spherical and one was a smaller cylinder. The liquid they were designed to hold would become millions of cubic feet of inflammable gas.

The tanks shown here were built by the East Side Gas Company in Cleveland in 1940. Here, they were still burning as a result of an explosion which occurred at 2:50 p.m. on October 20, 1944.

Many victims of the disaster were trapped under the shambles left by the exploding gas tanks. Workers searched among the debris for charred bodies.

After its original construction, one of the tanks, called a ''holder,'' had developed a small leak during tests. Repairs were subsequently made and the tank was tested again, this time proving satisfactory.

At 2:50 p.m. on the 20th, one of the gas tanks exploded, sending a sheet of flames over a very heavily-populated district. The fire made a shambles of the area stretching from the East Side north of St. Clair Avenue between East 55th and East 66th Streets—roughly a half mile square.

The Cleveland Fire Department, headed by Fire Chief James E. Granger, answered the call to fight the blaze. Ninety-five per cent of the force turned out in response to the multiple alarm.

Since the fire was in a highly-populated area, many people were forced to leave their homes. Residents of the district were alerted to the danger by loud-speakers which warned:

''The neighborhood is on fire! Get out! Run eastward!''

Mothers carrying young children ran out of flaming houses. Motorists left their automobiles on the street to run to safety. Some people even ran to Lake Erie to escape the raging fire.

Army, Navy, and Coast Guard personnel aided the firemen and police in fighting the conflagration. Ambulances carried the injured to nearby hospitals; approximately 200 people were treated. The Red Cross worked indefatigably. At least 1,500 people had been left homeless and in need of food and shelter.

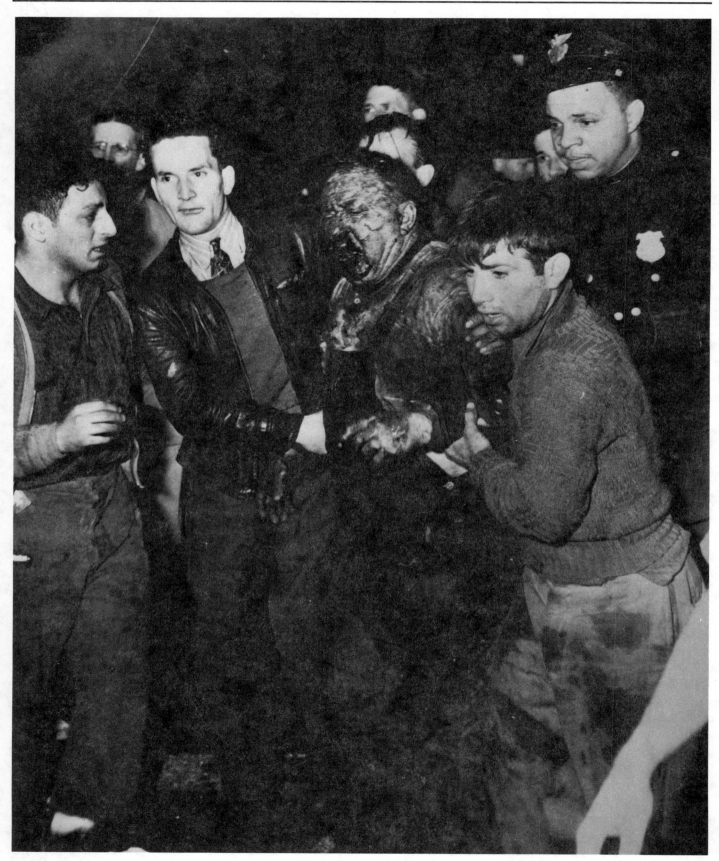

The explosion, which took place in a highly-populated area, left many residents homeless. Here, an unidentified man is being helped from the scene.

The effects of the blast were felt within a thirty-block radius of Cleveland. Even the manholes blew up from the explosion.

The fire continued to rage into the night. Heavy manhole covers were literally blown out of the streets by the force of the gas and flames. Broken gas mains emitted a blue flame which continued to be seen for the better part of a week. Devastation was so severe that, in addition to the people pulled from the wreckage, the birds flying over the area dropped to the ground, dead from the intense heat.

Activity in the city of Cleveland was brought to a halt by the explosion at the East Side Gas Company. As *Time* magazine stated on October 30:

''Production in Cleveland's war plants was halted.''

The total of known dead from the explosion and fire which resulted was 121. Eighty-two people were listed as missing and 1,500 were homeless. At a time when ration stamps were needed for food and clothing, the Red Cross managed to provide both for the survivors.

Was the cause of this terrible explosion a leak in an already faulty tank? The owners of the East Side Gas Company refuted this notion. Was the explosion caused by sabotage? This, too, remains an unanswered question. Whatever the cause, the results were devastating. The huge area greatly resembled the bombed-out sections of war-torn Europe. The East Side of Cleveland took much time to recover from that day.

When the French freighter, the Grandcamp, caught fire and exploded, it unfortunately helped to set off other explosions in the "Port of Opportunity"—Texas City, Texas.

Texas City, Texas, was known as the "Port of Opportunity." It's population had increased from 5,000 people to 15,000 during World War II. It was indeed a boom town—soon to be devastated beyond recognition.

On April 16, the *Grandcamp*—a converted French Liberty Ship—was being loaded with fertilizer to carry back to the farms in France. Twenty-three-thousand tons of fertilizer (made with ammonium nitrate and bagged in a highly flammable plastic) was lowered into the hold of the ship.

At 8 a.m. that morning, the ship's carpenter discovered some of the bags were on fire. No one was particularly alarmed when the report was turned in, and standard methods for putting out the blaze were instituted.

The *Grandcamp*'s captain, Charles de Guillebon, ordered the ship's smothering system into effect—a means of killing the fire with steam. Although this was a time-honored means of fighting flames on board, no one took into account the fact that the ammonium nitrate in the fertilizer would be turned into an explosive by the steam.

By 9:12 a.m., the *Grandcamp* disappeared in a cloud of smoke and flame; bodies were everywhere. Since the fire alarm had sounded long before the explosion, there were approximately 300 people standing on the dock watching—including many children who had not yet reported to school. Some of these people did not live to see another fire.

The Monsanto Chemical Plant collapsed totally from the force of the *Grandcamp*'s explosion, killing most of those who were inside. Nearby gasoline tanks also burst apart.

Twenty blocks of the waterfront and 12 blocks inland were totally obliterated. Two small airplanes circling 1,000 feet overhead were blown to bits by the blast, killing four occupants. Every window in Texas City was shattered by the force of the explosion.

The entire waterfront was ablaze. Warehouses, boats, buildings, and piers were reduced to rubble.

The United States Coast Guard arrived at the port to help fight the flames.

This close-up of the Monsanto Chemical Company plant shows the total collapse of the building which killed most of those who were inside.

Refineries and oil storage tanks burned heavy, black smoke as a result of the explosion.

Fire-fighting equipment was sent in from all over the area, but there was not much to be done except cleanup and help the living bury the dead. However, more devastation and loss of life were still to come.

Three ships had been tied up to Pier O. The *Grandcamp* had already exploded. The other two converted Liberty Ships were the *High Flyer* and the *Wilson B. Keene*. At 1:05 a.m. on April 17, the *High Flyer* exploded, tearing the *Wilson B. Keene* in half and causing many more deaths. This was the last major explosion at Texas City, although the fires were not fully extinguished for several days.

Five-hundred-and-fifty-two people died at Texas City; 3,000 more were injured and 200 were missing. The property damage exceeded $100 million.

The irony of this tragic occurrence, however, is that the National Maritime Union meeting was warned about Texas City just 36 hours before the fires and explosions broke out. James Gavin told union members that Texas harbor was ripe for disaster. This warning, though, was too little and too late.

Some houses were smashed as a result of the explosion at Texas City. The death toll was 552, while the number of injured was approximately 3,000.

Perseverance in the Face of Disaster

The Japanese who live on Honshu Island are unfortunately accustomed to floods. They have learned to persevere in the face of disaster; after the waters recede, they rebuild their homes and go on living. However, in the flood of September 20, 1947, about 1,000 people lost their lives in the swirling waters, while thousands more were listed as either missing or injured.

The flood waters rose in the wake of a typhoon. In Tokyo alone, they covered about 20 square miles of the city's eastern end—swelling as high as 15 feet before finally receding into the sea.

The streets of Tokyo were covered with so much water from the overflowing streams in the area that highways became waterways for boats. Those who could packed all of their belongings into their boats and traveled to higher ground.

This Tokyo street on Honshu Island was covered with so much water from the flood-swollen streams that the highways became waterways for boats.

Students from Koryo College helped rescue victims of the five-day flood which jeopardized life and property for thousands of people.

EPILOGUE

The Endurance of a People

American occupation forces still in Japan after World War II did what they could to help those who survived. One newspaper account said that thousands of marooned Japanese were saved by troopers of the United States First Cavalry Division.

Students from Koryo College also volunteered their services, and there were thousands upon thousands of people who needed help desperately.

When the rain ceased and the flood waters ebbed, the inhabitants of Tokyo and Honshu Island began their reconstruction. Indeed, the September flood of 1947 serves to highlight the endurance of a people.

A group of children were killed instantly when the Cathedral at Ambato caved in. These were only some of the estimated 6,000 who died as a result of the earthquake.

The earthquake began officially at 2:10 p.m. on August 5. A 1,500 mile area along the eastern Andes mountains was affected by the quake, and the death toll numbered more than 6,000 people; another 20,000 suffered injuries. Approximately 100,000 survivors were left homeless—and such towns as Ambato, Pelileo, Latacunga, Banos, and Patate were reduced to rubble.

Tremor Signals Impending Disaster

As devastating as these figures are, they would have been worse had there not been several warning tremors just before the quake struck full force. Heeding the warning tremors, residents in fifty towns ran into the streets minutes before buildings collapsed into rubble and debris.

The earthquake was no respecter of age or place. Children who were receiving religious instruction in the Cathedral at Ambato were killed when the Cathedral's roof caved in. The reverend who was teaching them became wedged under a fallen altar. However, four days later, rescuers found him still alive.

Natives gathered what little remained of their belongings at this destroyed town of Pelileo.

Homes were flattened to the ground by the earthquake which officially began at 2:10 p.m. along a 1,500 mile area in the eastern Andes mountains.

An Indian woman was holding her child in her arms when the earthquake hurled her into a yawning fissure. She lifted her baby as far over her head as she could. The earth closed over her, but the baby, held above the rubble by a dead mother's arms, was still alive when help came.

The town of Pelileo was reduced to nothing but rubble. Landslides from the surrounding mountains created piles of debris as high as 12 feet. Prior to the earthquake, the town numbered 3,500 people. Fewer than 1,000 survived. Pelileo sank 20 feet and suffered flooding from

This church was once located in the town of Cevellos and is only part of the devastation which occurred along the main street of the town.

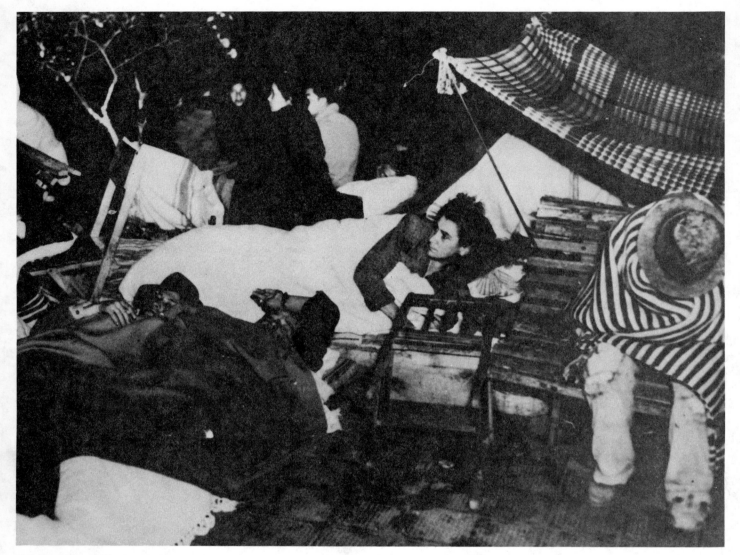

The residents of Ambato were forced to camp out in the streets with whatever they could find to protect them from the night air. The world quickly sent help to the stricken survivors.

what had once been a beautiful river. Those who were alive were forced to eat whatever they could find, and conditions remained primitive for days until help arrived.

The world moved quickly to help the stricken people of Ecuador. Neighboring countries responded to the need with airlifts, and the United States sent both supplies and Red Cross teams.

After the quake, which measured 7.5 on the Richter scale, the cleanup began. None of those who survived this disaster will ever forget the horror of the day the earth opened up in August of 1949.

WHEN THE BIG MUDDY BURST ITS BANKS

Weather experts warned of potential trouble in Kansas as early as May of 1951, for that was the wettest month in the recorded history of the state. June brought still more rain. The water-soaked land poured a two-month accumulation of rain into the Missouri River. The swollen waterway was dubbed the "Big Muddy" by those people who lived nearby.

200,000 Residents Evacuate Their Homes

Residents of the area were warned of the approaching flood and 200,000 left their homes before the raging water came. There were only 41 fatalities resulting from the flood, but property damage reached close to one-billion dollars.

In Kansas City, three major industrial districts went under water by the middle of July. Fire now added to the destruction caused by the rampant Missouri River. Storage tanks filled with gasoline, diesel oil, and naphtha exploded, pouring their contents on top of the flood waters. Although firemen worked around the clock, it took four long days to control the blaze.

Record-breaking floods followed in the wake of a raging river. Here, the Rock Island railroad yards in Kansas City, Kansas, are shown under water.

Fire was added to the destruction caused by the rampant Missouri River. Here, firemen fight the flames at a flooded fuel tank depot. The gasoline, diesel oil, and naphtha, which were contained within, had exploded and burned furiously in Kansas City, Missouri.

Kansas City had a population of approximately 900,000 people, and the water supply for these people was threatened. All nonessential businesses were ordered closed by Mayor William E. Kemp. Here, in Kansas City, a greater number of people were involved with the flood than in any of the other areas affected.

All along the watershed of the Missouri River, the rath of the flood was felt. Bridges were washed out; airports went under water; railroad tracks were flooded.

The *El Capitan*, a transcontinental train, was stranded near Wichita with 337 passengers aboard for more than 55 hours. Supplies and water were brought to the train by air. Bill Brandt, whose ranch was in Burns, Kansas, made fifteen trips in his plane, bringing what he could and transporting ill passengers to safety.

Drinking water was one of the worst problems for those in the flood area. Pure water had to be strictly rationed and was frequently trucked in to those in need.

Topeka, Kansas, was also flooded when the ''Big Muddy'' burst its banks. Here, a gasoline storage tank caught fire above the flood waters.

Power failures were the cause of what was called "Operation Pork Chop"—a project designed to deliver twenty-five million pounds of meat to the stricken areas. The major packing companies such as Armour, Swift, Wilson, and Cudahy removed the meat in their warehouses by boats to waiting refrigerated trucks.

Ten thousand head of livestock were evacuated to higher ground. About 850,000 acres of harvest-ready wheat and corn were covered by water. Although there was comparatively little loss of life, the economy of the area in the wake of the flood was in desperate straits.

Federal funds of $25,000,000 were provided by the United States Congress on July 18. President Harry S. Truman, who had made a personal tour of inspection, signed the bill passed by Congress and financial aid was on the way. In addition to money, the entire country sent

This aerial photo shows the flooded city of Kansas City, Missouri from the other side of the Kansas River. The area shown includes about nine square miles.

Volunteer workers laid down sand bags at New Haven, Missouri, to protect the fields beyond. Property damage from the flood and fires which followed was estimated to be nearly a billion dollars worth.

supplies to the flood-stricken area. Food and clothing were rushed in by the Red Cross and the Department of Agriculture; water-purifying units were sent by the Public Health Service.

Nearly a billion dollars worth of damage was done by the swollen Missouri River. In addition to the state of Kansas, Oklahoma and Missouri suffered from the flood. The property damage to cities and farmlands alike make this flood of 1951 the most destructive in the history of the area.

THE DEATH THROES OF THE U.S.S. HOBSON

April 26, 1952

The U.S.S. *Hobson* and her sister ship, the *Rodman*—a destroyer-minesweeper—were traveling through heavy seas on the night of April 26, 1952. Their mission was to escort the giant aircraft carrier, the U.S.S. *Wasp,* to the Mediterranean. The smaller ships were acting as look-outs in case any of the *Wasp's* airplanes had to ditch.

The *Hobson's* captain, Lieutenant Commander William J. Tierney, and a skeleton crew manned the bridge. The entire crew numbered 236 men, most of whom were already asleep.

Captain Burnham C. McCaffree was the skipper of the *Wasp*. A violent shift in wind direction caused Captain McCaffree to steer the *Wasp* into the wind. This was done so that his last flight of planes could land safely. The time was 10:30 p.m.

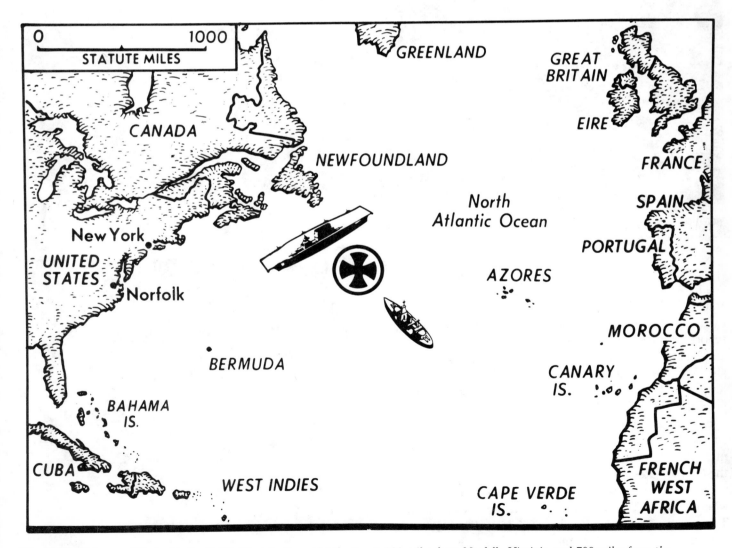

The U.S.S. Hobson collided with the U.S.S. Wasp in the mid-Atlantic—1,200 miles from Norfolk, Virginia, and 700 miles from the Azores. In a matter of minutes, the Hobson, with a large section of her bow ripped open, sank.

This lifeboat carrying some of the Hobson's survivors, is being hoisted aboard the carrier Wasp after the collision. Only 61 men were rescued.

The *Rodman* noted the *Wasp's* change in course and adjusted accordingly. Subsequent naval reports differed as to the actions of Lieutenant Commander Tierney. One report claimed that he ordered ''left rudder,'' while another stated that the *Hobson* did not change course at all. Whichever was the case, the fact remains that the huge *Wasp* rammed directly into the smaller vessel, breaking the *Hobson* in half.

Even the immediate reversal of the *Wasp's* engines could not help the crippled *Hobson*; in a matter of minutes, she went down. Those watching from the *Wasp* and the *Rodman* stood by completely helpless.

Sixty-one men were rescued from the oily waters where the *Hobson* sank. Lieutenant Commander Tierney, however, was not one of the survivors. For this reason, the naval board of inquiry summed up Tierney's actions by saying:

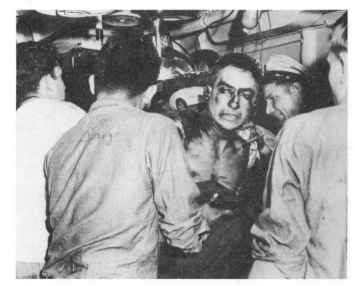

The minesweeper, Rodman, also rescued some of the survivors of the Hobson. The face of the man shown here reflects the harrowing experience he had just gone through.

Oil-covered survivors were picked up by the Wasp, which had rammed directly into the smaller vessel.

The Wasp entered Gravesend Bay at the lower entrance of New York Harbor. A large section of her bow was ripped open at the waterline, showing the damage of the collision at sea.

Navy divers had to go underwater to see the total damage to the Wasp. Although she suffered damage from the collision with the Hobson, there was no loss of life aboard.

"As the commanding officer was not among the survivors, his reasons for turning left will never be known."

The Navy placed the collision at 1,200 miles from Norfolk, Virginia, and 700 miles from the Azores. The *Wasp*, with a large section of her bow ripped open, had to turn back. Because of the 75 foot gash in her hull, the carrier took 11 days to limp home to Gravesend Bay at the lower entrance of the New York harbor. But the *Wasp* did get home; the *Hobson* wasn't that lucky.

In the quaint, little village of Belen de Las Flores—approximately 15 miles southwest of Mexico City—old-fashioned wooden streetcars were the mode of transportation to and from the city.

The people who boarded the trolley car on the clear evening of February 21 had no idea of the danger that awaited them. None of these passengers were going to be the same at the end of the evening.

The newspaper account of the accident stated that two wooden streetcars collided at high speed, resulting in the death of over 60 people and injuring 90 others. The site of the mountain grade where the two cars met was covered with wooden debris and strewn with bodies.

A head-on collision of two wooden street cars and the fire which followed resulted in the death of over 60 people; 90 more suffered injuries.

According to Major Luis Rodriguez, the head of the fire department, the cause of the crash was the fault of one of the streetcar drivers. Apparently, the driver failed to stop at a red light. It is possible that his brakes did not hold.

Since both of the streetcars were made of wood, fire broke out and the flames destroyed both cars.

Victims of the crash were rushed to the hospital for care, and rescue workers continued to search for bodies well into the wee hours of the night. This was reported as the worst trolley car accident in the history of Mexico City.

This aerial picture shows the broken Tangiwai Bridge and the tangled wreckage of the Auckland Express. The train crashed to its doom in the river below.

A Geography Lesson

A geography lesson about New Zealand would place Mount Ruapehu above the valley of the Whangaehu River. In the center of the last crater of Mount Ruapehu, one of New Zealand's North Island volcanos, is a beautiful lake. This lake is the source of the Whangaehu River.

151 Die Christmas Eve

In order to understand what caused the train crash at Tangiwai, the geography of the area must be explained. The eruption of Mount Ruapehu caused the death of 151 people on Christmas Eve in 1953, when it violently spewed forth water, mud, and rock.

As this great stream cascaded down the mountainside, large quantities of volcanic ash from an earlier eruption were absorbed into the flow. Trees, boulders, and ice were also swept up, and the result was what scientists call a "lahar." A lahar is a fearsome mudflow with force enough to ride over anything in its way.

The Tangiwai Bridge, built in 1906, stood 35 feet above the riverbed. Its construction was steel on concrete piers, and it was considered sturdy enough to withstand any normal occurrence. However, as the lahar came roaring down from Mount Ruapehu, it mangled the steel and concrete bridge as if it were a child's toy.

The express from Wellington to Auckland was due to travel the Tangiwai Bridge shortly after 10:21 p.m. Postmaster Cyril Ellis had heard the noise of the angry river and went out to investigate. Armed with a powerful electric flashlight, he saw that the river was 20 feet above normal.

Using his flashlight as a signal, Ellis waved to the Auckland Express to try to avert certain disaster. Although the driver of the great express saw the signal and heard Ellis' cry, he could not stop the train until it was almost at the middle of the bridge. The weight of the train was the final straw that broke the bridge in half.

The locomotive fell into the torrent below, pulling the first five cars of the train with it. All those inside drowned instantly. The sixth car of the train seesawed

Silt from the flood had to be removed from the cars of the train. This section was still sunk in the mudflow, when the rescuer began his work.

The locomotive and the cars shown here left the rails on the south side of the river and were hurled across the river by the force of the mudflow.

Only the metal frame of this car remained after the train, which was headed for Auckland, jumped the tracks. The number of lives lost in this train crash was 151, and all of Australia mourned their deaths.

precariously on the broken edge of the bridge. Warned by the watching postmaster, those inside that car tried to make their way to safety. However, there was no time. The joining which had held the sixth and seventh cars together broke; the car rolled over and over until it finally rested on the river bank. Some of those passengers were rescued.

In addition to the force of the current, oil from the oil-tender which had crashed first rose to the top of the water, making it even harder for any who survived to reach safety. Indeed, some of the people who did make

their way to the river banks were totally naked as their water- and oil-soaked clothes were ripped off of them.

Many tales of heroism came forth from the awful wreck of the Auckland Express. Four men, including Cyril Ellis, were honored by the newly-crowned Queen Elizabeth who was in New Zealand for a royal visit. The young Queen, as well as the entire country, was shocked at the train crash in which 151 people lost their lives.

There was no one to be blame for the catastrophe. It was just a cruel hand dealt by fate that placed the Auckland Express in a situation of despair.

ANDREA DORIA

The *Andrea Doria* was an Italian passenger liner measuring 697 feet long and 11 decks high. She was a 29,000 ton ship powered by huge twin turbine engines. On July 25, 1956, she was preparing for the final lap of her 51st crossing from Genoa to the United States.

The night was foggy, but such conditions were not uncommon in the waters just off Nantucket. Some passengers were preparing for the landing the next morning, while others were still enjoying the festivities of their last night at sea. Whether they were dancing in the lounge or packing in their staterooms, all of the passengers were shocked by the terrible shuddering of the ship which occurred about 11 p.m.

30 Foot Gash in Hull

In the fog, the bow of the Swedish American liner, the *Stockholm*, had plowed directly into the starboard side of the *Andrea Doria*. The terrific impact cut right through the *Andrea Doria's* hull, leaving a 30 foot gash. Tons of water poured into the damaged ship and she immediately listed to the right.

The Andrea Doria listed badly after her collision with the Stockholm, a Swedish liner, in the Atlantic Ocean near Massachussetts. This picture was taken aboard the Ile de France, which hurried to the rescue of the stricken liner.

The Italian ship sank into the sea 50 miles south of Nantucket. Today, the site is marked with a yellow buoy.

Lifeboats from the Andrea Doria were picked up by rescue ships. Over 1,600 people were plucked from the sea.

The captain and many members of the crew were the last to leave the stricken Andrea Doria.

Captain Piero Calamai had been using radar to steer the *Andrea Doria* on this last lap of her journey, but did not detect the *Stockholm*.

Due to the listing of the *Andrea Doria*, the lifeboats on the right side of the great ship were totally useless. However, the crew guided passengers safely to the lifeboats on the other side.

Captain Calamai immediately ordered an SOS distress call to be sent. The ships which answered that call were the *Tomas*, the *Cape Anne*, and the *Ile de France*. All of these ships—plus the *Stockholm*—conducted a rescue effort which was magnificent. Over 1,600 people were rescued from the *Andrea Doria*. Of the fifty-two people that ultimately died, most were killed on impact.

On the morning of the 26th, Captain Calamai left his ship; at 10:09 a.m., the *Andrea Doria* was swallowed up by the sea. Her final resting place is 225 feet deep, 50 miles south of Nantucket. Today, this site is marked by a yellow buoy.

The Ile de France came into New York Harbor with over 700 survivors of the Andrea Doria. Waiting crowds cheered the rescue ship.

Cause Unknown

The custom at sea dictates that ships going in opposite directions have a definite pattern to follow. This is to avoid exactly the type of collision that occurred when the *Stockholm* rammed the *Andrea Doria*. No one can say what happened to the modern equipment carried by both ships on that July night. Neither ship saw the other on their radar screen and nothing was picked up on radio.

The actual blame for this accident was never pinpointed. Perhaps the only conclusion to be drawn from the sinking of the *Andrea Doria* is that man is still an imperfect vessel and cannot always control his own environment.

Smoke poured out of the Almacen Vida Department Store in Bogata, Colombia. The fire took 82 lives.

There were only nine days left until Christmas. The Almacen Vida, a department store in Bogota, Colombia, was gaily decorated for the coming holiday and bustling with shoppers. Although counters displayed tempting gifts for the entire family, it was the toy department that was truly captivating. It was resplendent with a vast array of everything a child could want—many of those things made out of plastic.

A manger scene, complete with the figure of Baby Jesus lying in the straw, was highlighted with a string of brightly-colored lights. Unfortunately, it was these lights that caused the department store fire on that December day and took the lives of 82 people; 50 more were injured.

Christmas lights are well-known as possible fire hazards—and this particular string of colored lights was no exception. The fire began with a short circuit in the lights which set the straw under the Christ child ablaze. Nearby plastic toys began to burn and the fire spread rapidly to other counters in the toy department.

Despite the efforts of firemen and volunteers, the Christmas shopping ended in sadness for many. In addition to the number of dead, 50 more people suffered injuries.

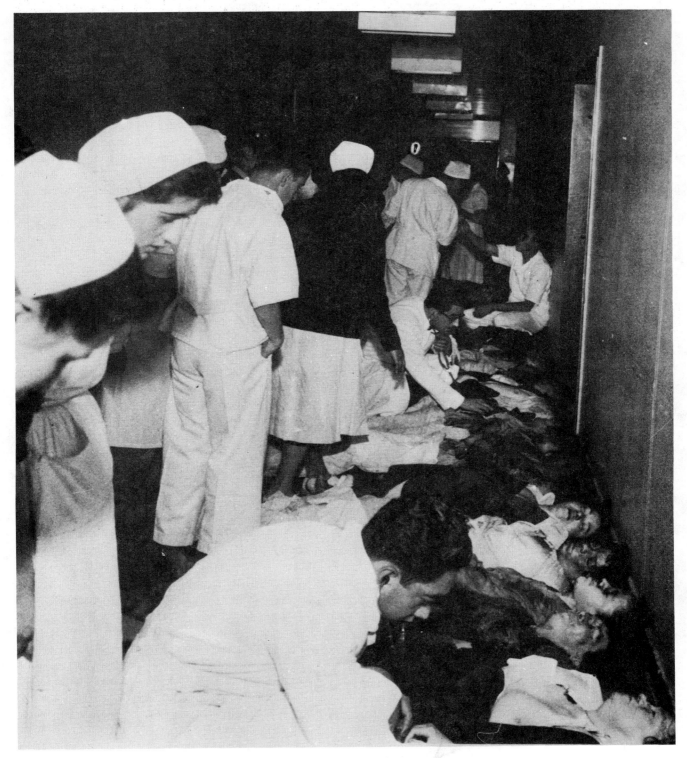

Victims lined up along hospital corridors, received prompt attention from doctors and nurses.

People began to panic as the smoke and flames spread. Although there was a rush toward the store's front exit, the frightened people were met there by the shooting flames. Clear-thinking men broke the glass showcase windows of the storefront and many escaped death by running through the broken glass.

Eighty-two people were trapped in the rear of the store, cut off by the fire in front and no exit door in back. None of these people survived. Indeed, fire, panic, and a string of colored lights created havoc in Bogota, Colombia, on December 16, 1958.

When the Earth Swallowed a City
The End of the U.S.S. Thresher
A Two Plane Crash
One Huge Mortuary Beneath a Sea of Mud
And Watts Burned
The Day the Earth Buckled
The School Children Who Never Grew Up
The Rampage of the Arno River
When the World Cried for Peru
Death at the Yarra Bridge
A Lady Named Agnes
A Fire Eleven Stories off the Ground
Turkish DC-10 Crash Near Paris
"It looked Like an Atom Bomb!"
Cause of the Crash — Unknown
8.2 on the Richter Scale
Planes Collide on the Ground
The Burning of a Supper Club
Flooding at Toccoa Falls
Massacre at Guyana
The Disaster that Almost Was
The Day the DC-10 Crashed at Chicago
The Rains of Death
A Capricious Sea at Fastnet Rock
Fire at the MGM Grand Hotel
Devastation in Southern Italy

WHEN THE EARTH SWALLOWED A CITY

Ruined buildings were all that were left on this street in Agadir, Morocco, after earthquakes struck the area.

During the last two weeks of February, 1960, the area surrounding the city of Agadir, in Morocco, had experienced several small earth tremors. The city, a prospering seaport and tourist resort, had a population of 48,000—mostly consisting of Moslems, Jews, and Christians.

Holiday of Devastation

Few people in Agadir paid any attention to the tremors. They reasoned that because the Moslems were celebrating the third day of a religious holiday, God would not harm them. There was surely nothing to fear.

This holiday, called *Romadan*, was celebrated by fasting in the daytime and feasting at night. Therefore, on the night of February 29, more people were up than usual: The Moslems were praying and feasting, and the tourists were enjoying the holiday atmosphere.

Near 12 a.m., the earth moved. In 12 brief seconds, the entire city of Agadir first moved four feet in one direction and then moved back. The city was devastated and seventy percent of all buildings were demolished.

Communication systems were out. It would be many hours before help would arrive. Every avenue and street was filled with stones, brick, and wood where once stood homes, businesses, and hotels.

Terror and pain filled the night. Cries for help were heard from within the rubble. Parents screamed to find children; husbands screamed to find wives. Sleeping couples were buried beneath mounds of stone. More than 70 Moslems, praying for guidance, were buried beneath the dome of their mosque.

Thousands of rats scrambled to the streets from broken sewers, spreading disease and filth. Although fires were

Citizens walk through the rubble and debris which had once been houses, businesses, and hotels.

The earthquake devastated the modern Saada Hotel, leaving only a broken sign over what had once been a resort retreat for visitors. Of the 150 guests who were staying there, 130 died in the quake.

burning out of control, the fire stations were no longer standing. All electricity was out.

The death toll mounted dramatically. Of the 150 guests staying at the modern Saada Hotel, only 20 survived. In the city's Jewish section, more than half of the 2,000 residents were crushed beneath stone and brick. Over 70 percent of the buildings in the Moslem quarter, the Talborjt, were razed.

French soldiers, sailors from the U.S. 6th Fleet, and the Moroccan Army began an enormous rescue effort. The open sewers reeked, and the dead and decomposing bodies added to the stench. DDT and quicklime were

sprayed everywhere to help fight disease and mask the odor.

The airport, miraculously left unscathed by the disaster, became a combined hospital and mortuary. From there, the injured were airlifted to other towns—some as far as 100 miles away.

After more than four days of digging, 4,000 bodies were found. Estimates indicated that 6,000 more people were still under the crushed buildings. Agadir was quarantined.

Miracles did happen though. An American Air Force family was staying in the Saada Hotel when the earth-

Private homes, like this once beautiful villa, became empty halls and sometimes burial mounds for the people who were trapped within.

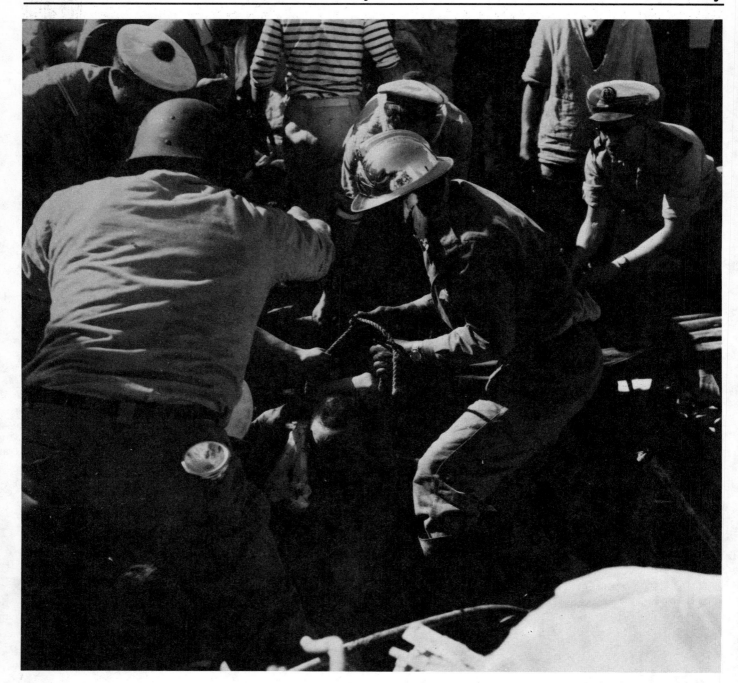

This moslem survivor of the quake was hauled unconscious from the ruins of a building. Although he lost an arm, the man lived—thanks to the efforts of the rescue team.

quake hit. The husband and infant child, buried together, were rescued after 14 hours of digging. The wife, never losing faith, was discovered still alive after being under the rubble of the hotel for almost 18 hours. In their attempts to rescue this woman, French soldiers had to dig through the hotel's roof and two stories to save her. It took over 40 hours until all three were reunited.

Disposal of the dead was a problem. Moslems and Jews had strict traditions for burying their dead. Each sect was quite distressed over the mass graves that were being used. The bodies, numbering more than 12,000, were sprinkled with disease-retardant lime and buried as soon as possible. Prevention of illness was more important than religious traditions.

The Moroccan King, Mohammed V, promised to donate his fortune of over $100 million to the reconstruction of Agadir. However, for the hundreds of survivors, money meant little. For them, the day the earth swallowed their city could not be erased by money, new buildings, or even time.

A TWO PLANE CRASH

December 16 was the beginning of the last weekend before the Christmas holiday. Busy shoppers were anxiously searching for just the right gift for that special someone. Families were preparing for a big Christmas celebration. Trains, planes, and buses were filled with travelers coming home for a snowy Christmas.

On that Friday, Trans World Airlines Flight 266 was scheduled to leave Dayton, Ohio for Manhattan's La Guardia airport. The four-engine propeller plane carried a crew of five and a passenger list of 39.

The captain was David Wollam. He was an experienced pilot with more than 14,500 hours of flying time. Captain Wollam informed his passengers that they would be flying at an altitude of approximately 7,000 feet and would reach New York in just over 1½ hours.

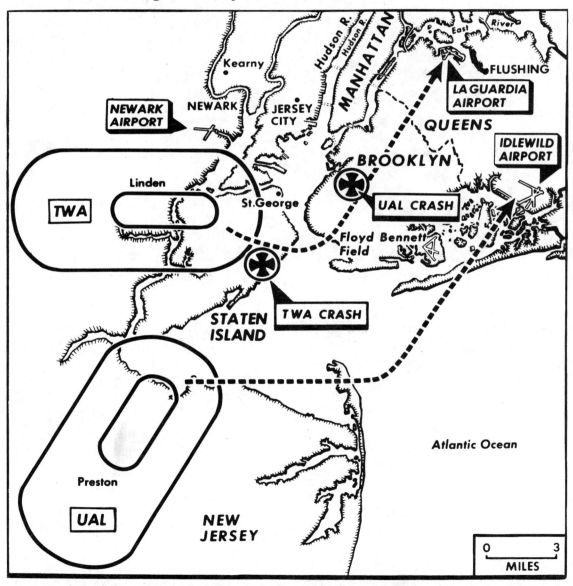

If normal stack-up patterns had been followed, the double tragedy of two planes crashing at different sites might have been avoided. No one at the site of either crash realized that there was a connection between the two.

People watched in horror as the tail section of the United Airlines plane fell to earth in Brooklyn.

A young family, traveling with their new-born infant, settled down for the short flight. The stewardesses made routine pre-flight checks. However, this flight was going to be far from routine.

Similar action was taking place aboard a United Airlines DC-8 at Chicago's O'Hare Airport. This plane, which held 76 passengers and seven crew members, was also bound for New York. It's destination, however, was Idlewild Airport in Queens.

On board this airplane was 11-year-old Steven Baltz of Wilmette, Illinois. He was planning to spend Christmas with his mother in New York. Steven and the other 82 passengers aboard the DC-8 had no notion of what lay ahead.

Both planes were following routine flight patterns. Idlewild (later renamed Kennedy) and La Guardia were monitoring these planes and received constant radio transmissions from them.

Suddenly, the sky began to rain death and terror. The TWA jet started to fall. The plane, breaking into three pieces, crashed into an Army base landing field in Staten Island. The plane narrowly missed two schools and several homes.

Soldiers rushed to the stricken jet. Although five people were rescued from the downed plane, all died before they reached the hospital. Forty-four people had been killed.

While housewives near the Army field watched the TWA jet fall, a shopkeeper in downtown Brooklyn was experiencing a similar horror. As Steven Baltz was later quoted:

". . .all of a sudden there was an explosion. The plane started to fall. . .and people started to scream. I held onto my seat. . ."

Firemen at the scene combed through the debris in search of bodies of the passengers as well as those in the nearby burned-out buildings.

Emergency equipment and rescue workers rushed through the snow-covered streets to help the living. It took more than two hours for over 250 firemen to control the fires.

Wreckage from the United Airlines plane was scattered over a square-mile area. Fire and debris were everywhere. The plane crashed directly into the Pillar of Fire Church and destroyed it. Jet fuel caused a six-story tenament and several shops and offices to burn. It took more than two hours for over 250 firemen to control the blaze.

All of the jet's 83 people, except one, died in the crash. Steven Baltz was found crawling out of the burning plane, his clothes on fire. He was rushed to a nearby hospital where a medical team worked frantically to save his young life. But the fumes and smoke had done too much damage. Steven died the following day, December 17.

No one at the site of either wreckage knew that the two crashes were related. But the men at both air-control towers watched helplessly as the tragedy unfolded on their radar screens. They saw the two planes melt into one image, one falling free of the other and off the screen. In Brooklyn, 134 people, including six on the ground, lost their lives.

Investigators into the cause of this tragic, pre-holiday crash named human error as the cause. The DC-8 was not on course. For some unknown reason, it had left its intended approach pattern. In doing so, it ran right into the TWA plane as it neared La Guardia.

To add to the irony of this terrible air catastrophe was the death of little Steven Baltz. The day he died was the 57th anniversary of the Wright brothers' first successful airplane flight.

The Wright brothers saw only promise in their invention. They could not envision the potential horror and death that air travel would someday cause.

THE END OF THE U.S.S. THRESHER

When the U.S.S. *Thresher* was launched at Portsmouth, New Hampshire, in 1961, the Navy felt that this nuclear submarine was ''one of the most effective anti-submarine weapons in the Navy arsenal.'' The *Thresher* was 279 feet long and displaced 4,300 tons. During test runs a few months before her official launching, the sub went deeper into the ocean than any other American submarine. When she left Portsmouth, the *Thresher* carried sophisticated detection equipment and could travel deeper, faster, and more quietly than any other known submarine.

Early in 1963 the *Thresher* returned to Portsmouth for some overhauling. The work was completed, and on April 9, the submarine left the naval dockyard for a series of new tests. She was accompanied by an escort vessel, the *Skylark*.

Aboard the *Thresher* were 129 men under the command of Lieutenant Commander John W. Harvey. Of these men, 17 were civilians who were there to ensure that all systems on the *Thresher* worked as they should. The first day out, the *Thresher* went through her test dives without incident. The sub was in constant contact with the *Skylark*, and there was no reason to worry when tests were resumed on the morning of April 10.

The nuclear submarine U.S.S. Thresher looked like this at its launching in July, 1960. Three years later, the submarine was believed to have gone down with 129 men on board.

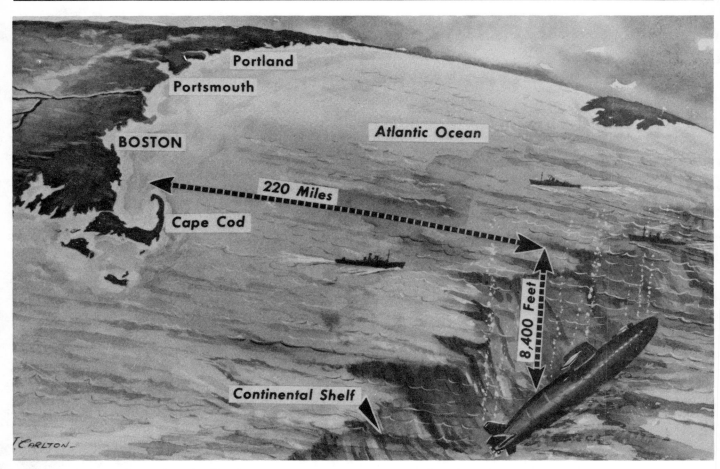

An artist's rendering shows where the Thresher was believed lost at the bottom of the Atlantic Ocean.

Memorial services for the lost crew of the Thresher were held at the Portsmouth Naval Shipyard in New Hampshire.

Six months after the Thresher went down, underwater pictures taken by the Department of Defense found the topside rudder of the nuclear submarine at a depth of more than 8,000 feet.

Wilkenson Deep, in the North Atlantic, is 220 miles east of Cape Cod off the coast of New Hampshire. At Wilkenson Deep on the morning of April 10, the U.S.S. *Thresher* dived below the surface. The time was 7:52 a.m. The sub reported to the *Skylark* that she was 300 feet deep.

A routine check for leaks was also carried out and reported to the *Skylark* on the surface. Communication from the *Thresher* to the *Skylark* continued at regular intervals until 9:02 a.m., when the submarine had reached a depth of 1,000 feet.

Trouble occurred a very short time later, and those aboard the *Skylark* could only listen helplessly to a garbled, hard-to-understand transmission—the last to be heard from the U.S.S. *Thresher*.

The men on the *Skylark* listened in vain. There was no response to their transmissions in Morse Code. There were no answers to the explosive signals the *Skylark* sent off. There was nothing to be seen when the *Skylark* circled the area looking for the missing nuclear submarine.

At 11:04 a.m., the *Thresher* was reported as missing. Several nearby submarines hurried to the area to join in the search. By late afternoon, all that had been found

were some yellow and red gloves of the kind used in the nuclear-reactor section of the submarine and some bits of plastic that seemed to indicate that the submarine had broken apart.

The families of the 129-man crew were notified that the *Thresher* was missing, but the Navy continued a fruitless search.

On June 20, 1963 the inquiry into the loss of the *Thresher* reached the assumption that a failure in the saltwater piping system allowed flooding of the engine room. As a result of this failure, the *Thresher* exceeded its depth limit and fell to the ocean floor, 8,400 feet below. At this depth, the water pressure exerted on the submarine would have crushed it and all who were in it.

On August 29, the Navy sent down the bathysphere that found final evidence. Hunks of plate metal and what appeared to be submarine parts were seen. The bathysphere brought up a piece of piping on which the numbers 593 were engraved. This was indeed a part of the nuclear submarine called the U.S.S. *Thresher*, which went to its watery grave on April 10, 1963 with 129 men on board.

ONE HUGE MORTUARY BENEATH A SEA OF MUD

160   October 9, 1963

When the side of Mount Toc fell into the lake below it, water flooded over the top of the 873 foot Vaiont Dam into the valley below. The box in this picture shows where the force of the water tore away some of the concrete of the dam.

This gory headline, above, set in bold, black capital letters in an American newspaper, sums up the events that took place in Italy on October 9, 1963. Waters from the Vaiont Dam almost totally destroyed all of the towns in the valley below.

The Vaiont Dam, located in northern Italy, was one of five dams that supplied hydroelectric power to the Piave Valley below. The dam was a curved wall standing 873 feet above the valley and the Piave River.

Four years were spent building the dam, which was completed in 1960.

However, the lake behind the dam was not filled until two years later. Engineers were concerned about the condition of Mount Toc, the mountain on which the dam was built. There was reason for concern—cave-ins and cracks appeared in the mountain almost before the dam was completed.

Pirago, one of the five towns located in the valley was devastated. Only the tower of the town's church and some electric transmission poles were left standing.

After corrections had been made to the dam structure and the mountain was tested again, local authorities were assured that the dam was safe and there was little or no danger to the valley and towns below.

Early in the wet autumn of 1963, some people were concerned with the condition of the mountain on which the Vaiont Dam rested. Mount Toc rose to 6,000 feet, and its sides had been loosened by the continuous rains. Minor landslides were enough to worry the Mayor of Erto, located in the Pineda district. The mayor posted a notice to the citizens of his town warning them not to go near the shores of the lake. Even fishermen were asked to keep away.

There were about 4,000 inhabitants in the Piave Valley at that time. The villages along the valley were Longarone, Pirago, Rivalta, Villanova, and Fae. The people living in these small towns were in their homes on that night of nights. As midnight approached, many were asleep. Others were watching television or generally putting the finishing touches on their day.

Shortly before midnight, the whole side of Mount Toc fell into the lake below. The landslide, which loosened rocks and earth and even large trees, poured into the lake, displacing the water. Suddenly, a giant wave reared up from inside the lake and poured over the dam in a cascade that totally changed the face of the Piave Valley.

Two elderly women mourn their dead near the ruins of a village near Belluno.

The water became a tremendous torrent that swept away everything in its path.

Of the five villages located in the valley, none survived the awful waters. All but the very highest houses in these towns were wiped out of existence as if they had never been. The loss of life was approximated at 1,900. It was not possible to make a closer count because all local records from the towns had been washed away.

Those few who survived the overflow of the Vaiont Dam described what happened when a thunder-like noise seemed to fill the air. Survivors and authorities assumed that the great dam had burst. They thought the water that did so much damage had come from the lake as it burst through the concrete walls of the dam.

Later an investigation showed that the dam had not burst. The water that twisted pieces of metal into weird shapes and destroyed everything within its way was raised by the landslide or avalanche that came from Mount Toc.

Clean-up, which began the next day, continued for many days. Bodies were found tossed into the tops of tall trees. Other bodies were completely denuded by the force of the water; many were totally unrecognizable. The hundreds of tons of water that cascaded over the lip of the Vaiont Dam swept away everything in its path, leaving a veritable sea of mud where once there had been a peaceful valley.

As is the case in many disasters, a court of inquiry was set up after the fact. Was the location of the Vaiont Dam a safe site on which to build? Was the design of the dam at fault? Had local authorities taken enough care in watching the condition of Mount Toc itself? Could the

loss of life have been averted in any way? Although many of these questions provoked arguments on both sides, the Vaiont Dam was closed down.

The results of the avalanche created a new mountain peak rising out of the lake. What had once been a huge lake was now reduced to a small pool. There was no longer any danger to be feared from an overflow at Vaiont Dam.

Water was still pouring over the Vaiont Dam when this aerial picture was taken. Flood waters wiped out the five towns below the dam.

These salvage operations took place in the Longarone area. The total loss of life was only approximated, as all local records were washed away.

AND WATTS BURNED...

August 11–16, 1965

Perhaps the best description of Watts prior to 1965 was written by the *San Francisco Chronicle*. The *Chronicle* described the Watts area of Los Angeles as "a little like a pressure cooker." The pressure of poverty and all it entails, plus the steam of a hot, muggy summer caused an explosion that was to change a city in August of 1965.

Watts began as a black community before 1916. By the time the rest of America was enjoying the flapper era, Mud Town, as Watts was then known, was already a slum. It was over 98 percent black and was 100 percent poor.

The city of Los Angeles had grown and prospered around Watts. The mainly white, upper middle classes had built a city where people could shop, dine, and go to the theater without going through Watts. The Negro (a term widely used until after the civil rights riots of the '60s) was seldom seen outside of Watts. When he was seen, it was usually in his role as a domestic. In essence, the Negro was rarely seen and never heard.

The rioting in Los Angeles took place in a 35 square-mile area known as Watts. Police and the California National Guard were unable to control the burning and looting which took place.

This scene of destruction in the Watts area shows what remained of stores after the rioting had ceased.

Firemen and armed policemen struggled to control the arson-minded mobs.

Much of the racial intolerance in Los Angeles was divided among the immigrating Japanese and Mexicans as well as the Negroes. The years of the '60s were to change all this.

In early 1960, a new president was elected—a young man, full of promise and a member of a minority. He was a Catholic. He saw the racial inequalities in the American way of life and began to initiate legislative changes. His successor made these changes law. The Civil Rights Act of 1964 was full of hope for millions of people. It espoused racial equality and promised an end to discrimination on every level.

The residents of Watts in the summer of 1965 were hot and tired. They saw very little of the benefits promised them in 1964. They were still unemployed and lived in substandard housing. The pressure was rising.

On August 11, Watts exploded. It all began innocently enough when a white officer of the Highway Patrol arrested and charged a Negro man with drunken driving. A crowd congregated at the scene. Hundreds of Negroes

Buildings were broken into and looting of everything from liquor to lampshades took place. Ironically, the Negroes were destroying their own homes, cars, and stores.

Motorcycle police assembled in Watts to help manage the unruly crowds which threw bottles, rocks, and bricks.

taunted the police and threw rocks at them. One woman was sent to the hospital.

Tension and violence grew. Approximately 400 law-enforcement officers cordoned off a 20-block area of Watts, to contain the 5,000 rioting Negroes. Young blacks were firing on policemen. Cars were set afire. Buildings were being broken into, and there was much looting. Ironically, the Negroes were destroying their own homes, cars, and stores.

The white police chief was quoted as saying, most unsympathetically, that violence should be anticipated ''when you keep telling people they are unfairly treated.''

By August 13, the National Guard was brought into Los Angeles. Troops were armed with rifles, machine guns, bayonets, and tear gas. They were ordered to use whatever means necessary to stop the rioting.

Violence was spreading. The white suburbs of San Pedro and San Fernando were attacked. Hundreds of whites were evacuated. Damage to these predominantly white-owned areas was estimated at well over $10 million. Four people were killed.

On August 14, the city's Negro leaders were pleading for an end to the violence. Curfews were imposed on an area of Los Angeles covering 35 square miles. Twenty-one people were now dead. Airlines were asked to use alternate routes to avoid the sniping. The man whose arrest touched off this drama pleaded guilty to the charge.

The city was finally brought under control on August 16. The violence left more than 30 dead, and seven hundred people injured. Jails held more than 2,200 people arrested during the melee. More than 1,000 fires had been set. Property damage was estimated at over $200 million. Americans came face-to-face with the racial issue.

The biggest tragedy of Watts was not the loss of property but the fact that it took a disaster of this nature to bring about change.

An evaluation into the actual causes of Watts showed a grossly unequal education system between white and black residents. Blacks were far behind in educational levels. Among other recommendations was a one-third cut in the size of Negro classes.

Job-training and placement centers to reduce Negro unemployment were established. Negroes were being shown, many for the first time, that they could accomplish anything they really wanted to. A black man no longer had to be satisfied with cleaning a white man's home or shining his shoes.

The blacks in Los Angeles have come a long way in the years since Watts exploded. People of all races have learned from the fires lit in Watts that hope and action could rise from the ashes of racial discrimination.

This scene of one of Watts' main streets shows the effects of the fires which were started by the rioting mobs.

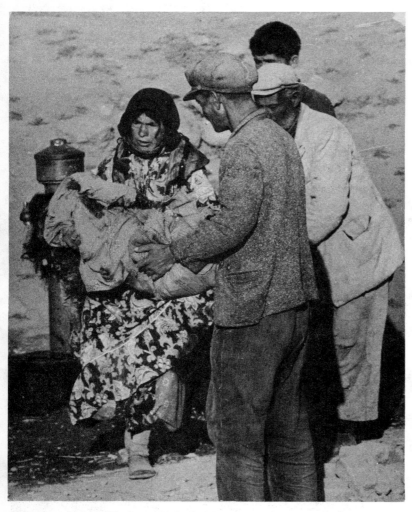

The town of Varto, Turkey, felt the full force of the earthquake. This mother, carrying her dead child, had only a few minutes to prepare the body before compulsive burial took place.

Turkish citizens live in a belt where earth tremors are not uncommon. They had suffered earthquakes before August 19, 1966, and they have had them since. But, on that Friday, a conservative estimate states that 2,500 people died and another 1,500 were injured. Four provinces in Turkey suffered damage from the quake, and 140 villages were destroyed.

The quake on August 19 was so intense and so severe that the entire world took notice and eventually sent help to the stricken people. Although the earth tremors were devastating in themselves, they did not cause the majority of deaths. Death came from falling buildings rather than the actual tremors of the earth.

Rescue teams of soldiers from Turkey's Third Army Corps were rushed to the scene. But they were hampered in their efforts to reach the site of the earthquake. The town which was hit the hardest was Varto, located about 450 miles east of Ankara. The poor roads leading to Varto were now further impeded by landslides and crevasses. It was slow going for the soldiers trying to reach the area as quickly as possible.

When the troops finally reached Varto, they were greeted with a scene of utter destruction. Working through the long night and guided only by flares and the cries of those who were trapped, they dug for survivors.

When dawn came, the extent of the horror was better able to be seen. Whole villages had been wiped out. Those who survived were attempting to locate missing members of their families—alive or dead. There was no food to eat and no water to drink.

As soon as possible, the relief agencies set up emergency hospitals and field kitchens. Thousands of people had to be fed. The clean up task was tremendous.

Still another problem confronted the residents of Varto and the surrounding areas. The danger of widespread cholera caused a need for immediate vaccination of more than 200,000 people.

The world responded quickly and generously to Turkey's plight. Supplies were sent from Great Britain and other European countries. America dispatched millions of dollars in aid to Turkey as well as medicines, food, and other relief supplies.

The people of Varto ultimately buried their dead, as did all of those in the surrounding villages. Despite the terrible events on the day the earth buckled, life went on. But, for about 2,500 people, the earthquake in Turkey proved to be the end of their world.

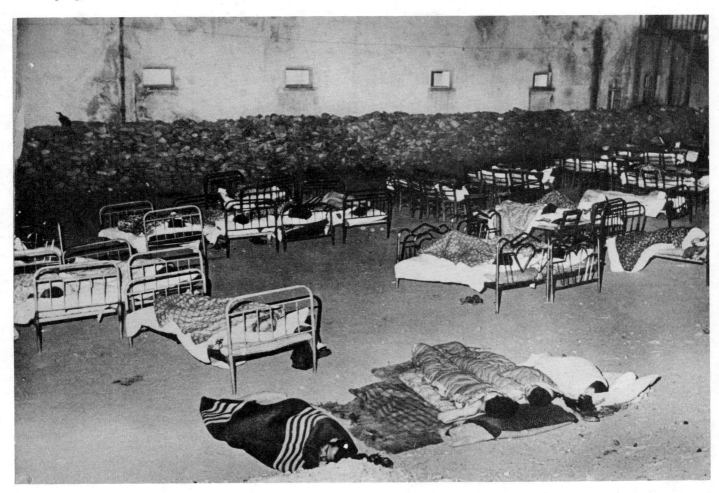

Those who survived were forced to sleep in the streets of Varto after the earthquake caused the death and destruction of the town.

THE SCHOOL CHILDREN WHO NEVER GREW UP

Aberfan, a small mining community in South Wales, was not always covered with coal dust. The name Aberfan means ''mouth of the River Fan,'' and until 1869 it was an unspoiled country community with tall trees, green grass, and wide, open fields.

Seven Tips of Slag

The first coal shafts were sunk near Aberfan at the Merthyr Vale Colliery in 1869. Houses were built close together on terraces to accommodate the miners and their families. As the years passed, huge piles of coal waste, called tips, became black mountains reaching as high as 80 or 90 feet into the air. By 1966, nearly 100 years later, there were seven tips of slag heaps. The oldest were sprouting green grass on top. The newest were less than half a mile from the village.

Thunder-Like Noise

The morning of Friday, October 21 seemed like any other school day to the 240 youngsters who were at their desks at Pantglas School. There may have been a little excitement in the air, because this was the last morning before the half-term holiday was to begin. The children, ranging from 4½ to 11 years old, were finishing up their work for the week.

The man-made mountain of slag in the background was loosed by an avalanche which crashed down on the Pantglas School in Aberfan. The death toll included 116 children and 28 adults.

Rescue workers, including police, civil defense workers, and parents rushed to the scene. They laid sandbags in the hopes of preventing further damage to the town of Aberfan.

Before anyone in the school had time to think, a thunder-like noise was heard. The sludge and liquid coal of tip number seven had started an avalanche that crashed and roared its way down the hillside and over the railway embankment. The avalanche reared up 30 feet into the air and rushed on into the village of Aberfan.

The Pantglas School was in the way of the moving mountain of sludge. The avalanche hit the school with terrific force, moved on through a row of houses, and finally came to a halt at the roofs of some houses on Aberfan Road. The terrible damage was done in less than 15 minutes.

Fire brigades arrived at 9:30 a.m. to face an unimaginable scene. Flooding water was pouring out of broken water mains. Flames leaped forth from the debris of broken buildings, and there was the fear of still more wreckage from new slides. The black mountain had moved at a terrible price for the people of Aberfan.

Police, civil defense workers, and miners rushed to the scene to help the town. Other volunteers responded to a call for help from the British Broadcasting Company. There was so much response that the narrow roads into Aberfan were soon clogged with people and vehicles trying to help.

Frenzied mothers and fathers began digging through the ruins of what had once been a school. Bucket chains were formed by other rescuers to move out the black sludge, while still others worked to tunnel into the aftermath of the avalanche.

At various times during the grizzly work, one of the policemen would blow a whistle to ask for silence so that everyone nearby could listen for any signs of life. No one was found alive after 11 a.m.

The work continued all through the day and on into the night. By 10 p.m., 60 bodies of children had been recovered. Some of the children were found under their

With a background of the slag heaps which caused the destruction, workers dig a communal grave to bury the dead.

The small caskets of children were laid to rest together. Grief-stricken relatives filed by.

desks, where they had been trying to protect themselves. Their dead bodies were removed from the debris. A teacher had attempted to shield some children with his own body—his attempts were unsuccessful.

One hundred sixteen children and 28 adults died in the avalanche at Aberfan. The press coverage of this disaster caused resentment from some of the grieving families, although for the most part the press tried to act with compassion. Still, their job was to tell the world what had occurred at Aberfan.

Most-resented of all was the National Coal Board, who owned the tip. Stories began to circulate that there had been trouble from tip number 7 before that October day in 1966. It was rumored that there had been trouble in January, 1964. In fact, the slag-heap had moved twice—once in 1959 and again in 1964. The National Coal Board had received more than one warning of the possible danger to Aberfan.

A Tribunal of Inquiry was set up under Lord Justice Edmund Davies. After hearing many hours of testimony from over 100 witnesses, the Tribunal concluded that the disaster at Aberfan could and should have been prevented. As a result of their findings, an Advisory Committee on Tip Safety was set up in 1968. No other avalanche of coal waste was going to be allowed to take lives.

This must have been of small comfort to the bereaved families of Aberfan. In a matter of minutes, a whole generation of children had been wiped out. Not even an Aberfan Disaster Fund, which ran to over one million pounds, could restore these children—the children who never grew up.

THE RAMPAGE OF THE ARNO RIVER

November 3–4, 1966

The rampage of the Arno River in Italy is a two-fold story. Raging flood waters devastated the valleys of the Po and Arno areas of the countryside. The waters destroyed 12,000 homes and farms. In the towns of the valley 10,000 homes were wiped out and bridges and communications were all destroyed. Farm equipment was damaged, livestock was killed and the death toll for people reached to over 100. Five thousand families were left homeless.

The weather that autumn brought unusually heavy rains to Italy, but the country was accustomed to floods. The world made little of the devastation to the Italian rural areas that were hurt at that time. However, the world was going to grieve for the cultural devastation that occurred to the city of Florence.

The Arno River runs directly through the city of Florence. The older part of the city is right on the river and is made up of fine old palaces and buildings that house priceless art treasures. When the river rose 18 feet higher than usual, the only place the water could go was into the city.

The streets of Florence were flooded by the Arno River. This square, in front of Santa Croce Basilica, was covered with mud and debris—stranding the cars that were there.

The helicopter flying over the flooded countryside around Florence is only one of many. The pilots made mercy trips carrying food and medicine to the stricken areas.

Slimy mud covered the steps of this school in Florence, which was transformed into a supply center where residents queued up for emergency supplies.

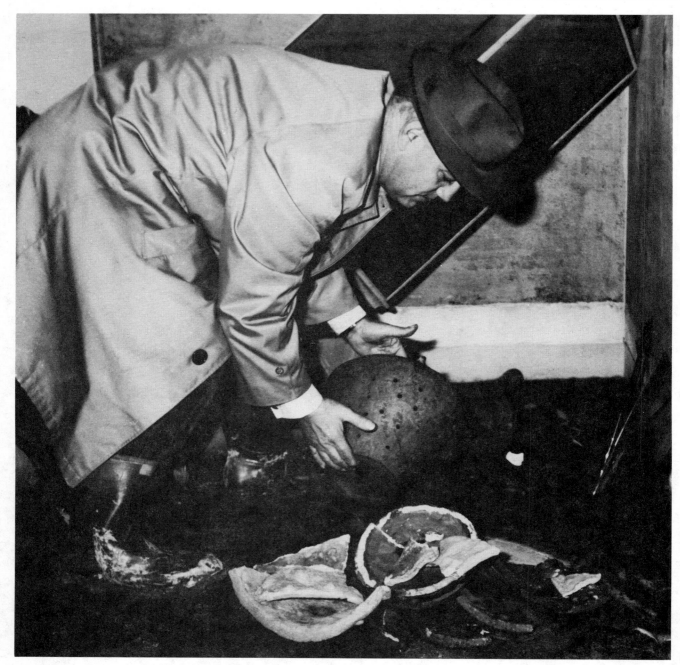

The director of the Etruscan Museum in Florence, Professor Guglielmo Maetzke, wears boots as he examines one of the priceless art objects that was damaged in the flood.

On November 3, cellars and basements in Florence were already filling with flood waters. The usually slow-moving stream, the Arno, had become a swirling mass of dirty water.

Some of the goldsmiths and jewelers who had shops in the old quarter on the Ponte Vecchio had such valuable wares in their shops that they kept night watchmen. When the watchmen saw the rising waters some of them notified their employers. Because of this, some shopkeepers were able to get to their shops and save some of their belongings from the greedy waters of the Arno. However, most of the people of Florence were not that lucky.

For 18 hours, the waters of the Arno raged through the city of Florence. Automobiles were tossed about like toys in water-covered streets. Basements and first floors became filled with the muddy water, which was no respecter of good or bad. The water despoiled irreplaceable art objects along with inexpensive souvenirs.

As the waters rose, Florentines worked frantically to move their belongings to upper floors of their homes.

The cultural loss which the flood of the Arno River caused in Florence could not be measured in dollars. Shown here are piles of books and documents from the Florence State Archives which suffered damage from the waters.

The people of the many art galleries in Florence made attempts to save the precious works that were stored below ground. Some oil paintings were saved in this way. Unfortunately, others were lost.

The Santa Croce Church had proudly displayed a Cimabue crucifix—a rare art piece considered one of the best works of the Byzantine artist. The crucifix was torn from its place in the church and carried away by the powerful mud and water. When it was later picked up out on the knee-deep mud, grown men cried at the cultural loss.

The famous doors of Ghiberti were damaged by the fast-moving waters. Irreplaceable paintings by the score were damaged in still another way. The water tore through basements and cellars, destroying central heating systems and adding oil, naphtha, and other chemicals to the muddy mess. When the flood finally receded, a thick black covering of mud and oil had done irreparable damage to the art it had covered.

Italy's National Library was located in Florence, containing thousands of rare books and manuscripts. Some of these had been sent to Florence from all parts of the world to be restored and repaired by the librarians there. Thousands of these rare books and manuscripts were damaged.

Although there was comparatively little loss of life in the Arno flood waters, the citizens of the city suffered from lack of food and shelter. Many faced the cold weather from the roofs of buildings until they could move down into a mud-covered city.

The world, however, was not concerned with people. Rather, the news that went out was about the tremendous loss of artwork. A cultural world responded with help as soon as it could. Students converged on Florence to aid in the mop-up, and experts were sent from many famous museums to lend a hand. People subscribed to the Italian flood fund, and Florence set about to prepare for her biggest business—tourism. By 1967, tourists were again coming to the famous art center.

Is it possible that this flood might have been avoided? When the waters had settled down from their mighty rampage, one more fact emerged. On November 3, the Italian Electricity Authority had opened the flood gates of Levane Dam—35 miles up-river from Florence. This action ensured that Florence would be flooded, and a warning was given to the city engineers. In a mistaken effort to avoid panic, no warning was issued to the citizens of Florence.

WHEN THE WORLD CRIED FOR PERU

Ocean Bed Cracks 50 Miles Off the Coast of Peru

It all began 50 miles off the coast of Chimbote, Peru—when the ocean bed cracked. This caused the earth to move and created an earthquake that was recorded between seven and eight degrees on the Richter scale.

The people of Peru had lived with the knowledge of bad earthquakes all through their history. However, the one that occured on May 31, 1970 covered a tremendous land area and took a death toll of thousands.

Estimated 30,000 Dead

The affected area of Peru was a 250-mile stretch of coast from Trujillo in the north to as far south as the capital city of Lima. People in Lima did not suffer the devastation that occurred farther north, and, owing to the lack of communication, they were not at first aware of what had happened. It was several hours later before the magnitude of the earthquake was realized.

The shock of the earthquake is reflected in this Indian woman's eyes. With her child on her back, she stares in disbelief at a collapsed cliff near Sayan, 60 miles north of Lima.

What was once the town of Casma was totally destroyed. This aerial photograph was taken after the massive quake.

Chimbote, a port city in Peru, was left in ruins. The hospital there was partially destroyed.

Rubble from the houses which once stood in Huaraz was piled high in the streets. The tremendous death toll resulted as much from the collapsed buildings as from the quake itself.

Radio communications were completely shut off because of damage to the hydroelectric station at Huallanca. Landslides made coastal roads totally impassable. Airfields were unusable. Because of the lack of communication, the amount of damage was only a guess.

Early reports stated that 2,700 people were dead at Chimbote. The town was in ruins. As other reports came in, it became known that towns all along the coast had suffered, and more thousands of people were dead.

General Velasco, the president of Peru, was forced to survey the damage to Peru in a naval vessel. The morning after the quake he inspected the damage to Chimbote—a total ruin—and to Casma and Coishco. When he returned to Lima, the president carried on board some of the people who were injured and in need of medical help.

However, the story was far from over. The coastal towns were only part of the damage caused as a result of the earthquake. The mountainous area of Callejón de Huaylas was completely cut off. Road travel was prohibited by rock-covered roads. Even planes and helicopters could not see, because of poor visibility and huge clouds of dust. No one knew what had happened to the town of Yungay and its neighbor, Ramrahirca. When word finally got out, it described more horror.

A landslide down the side of Mount Huascaran had swallowed up all of Yungay and part of Ramahirca. A huge wall of mud and snow had come down, covering and

Huaraz, one of the largest cities in this section of Peru, suffered the most damage. Here, three children are standing in the midst of all that was left of this street.

destroying people in the two small towns. Palm trees, once 100-feet tall, were just spots of green in what had been the main square of Yungay. These remote parts of the Andes mountains could not be reached for almost three full days.

There were, unbelievably, some spectators to the landslide down Mount Huascaran. A group of Japanese mountain climbers were 5,000 feet up the mountain. In horrified fascination, they watched the huge avalanche fall 10,000 feet down the face of the mountain. They actually witnessed the mass below them moving down on the valley at an incredible speed.

While many of the native Indian population died in the landslide, hundreds of thousands did survive—only to be faced with no heat, food, or shelter. People who suffered these deprivations died before help could reach them. It is estimated that 30,000 people died here.

Rescuers dug to find the living and the dead all up and down the coast of Peru. People tried to begin new lives, but they lived with the fear of more earth tremors. Many feared flooding from nearby mountain lakes, but this did not occur.

The world, as well as all parts of Peru, sent supplies to the stricken areas. Homeless people were helped to build temporary shelters. Food and clothing alleviated the serious condition for many.

Though the world tried to help, it was up to the people of Peru to rebuild, hopefully in such a way that a possible future earthquake could not do this same amount of damage. Only time will tell whether that hope will be realized.

This picture, taken almost a year after the earthquake, shows the remains of what once was a fine cathedral in Huaraz.

DEATH AT THE YARRA BRIDGE

The West Gate of the Yarra Bridge in Australia was being built to increase commercial trade between the cities of Williamstown and Fort Melbourne. Jack Hindshaw, resident engineer for the work, was worried. Six weeks earlier a buckle had been found under a span of the west end, and no corrections had been made.

Growing more concerned, Hindshaw called the contractor just before noon on October 15, asking for advice on how to correct the defect. His workmen, on their lunch break in huts below the ill-fated span, were unaware of any problems. As Hindshaw was returning from that telephone call, he heard a deafening roar. He looked up in horror to see the span of bridge, over 1,200 tons and 360 feet wide, collapse on his men.

A workman 160 feet above the Yarra River lived to describe what he saw:

The West Gate of the bridge across the Yarra River was being built to increase trade between Williamstown and Fort Melbourne. Shown here is the last span a few days before it collapsed.

Shown here are the remains of the span and column which collapsed into the muddy river. The workmen's huts which were located underneath were crushed.

"I felt it [the span] shaking but thought it was my imagination and kept on working . . . Then the whole damn thing sagged in the middle. I could see daylight through the enormous cracks in the concrete."

An alarm was called in, and rescue teams raced to the scene. Diesel oil, spilled during the crash, was burning. Mud, oil, and pieces of steel covered everything. Workmen, doctors, and priests worked frantically to save the injured construction crew.

Cranes were brought in to lift pieces of the span from injured or dead workmen. Bodies were everywhere; some were not recovered for days. In all, 35 men were killed—Jack Hindshaw was one of them.

An investigation was begun immediately. The reason for the bridge's collapse was found to be negligence.

The bridge was being constructed by the "box-girder" system. This is a series of prefabricated squares of girders that are attached to the open end of the bridge. The dangers in this method of building had already been proved twice—in Vienna in 1969 and again at Milford, Wales, just four months before the events at Yarra. Spans of those two bridges had collapsed, killing four people. If organization and communication systems are good, the use of this complex construction method can be economical and practical. Such was not the case at Yarra.

The people in charge of the over-all project were named by the Royal Commission with "failing to define areas of responsibility." The design consultants were responsible for only the steel sections and not for the design of the concrete sections. Construction was done by

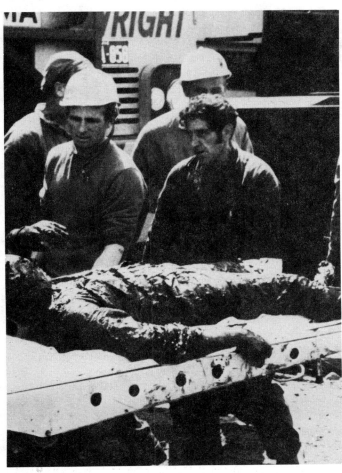

This mud-covered worker was only one of many who were injured when the West Gate Bridge collapsed.

yet another company. Two contractors were used. One company, a Dutch firm, had to stop working on the project in midstream. The new company, run by Hindshaw, did not report the first buckle until after many lives were lost.

Wherever the fault lay, it was too late to bring back the 35 men who lost their lives. However, an important lesson was learned from this disaster. The construction industry wrote into practice new methods, standards of construction, and construction procedures. Perhaps many more lives were saved on future construction sites because of the lessons learned at noon, October 15, 1970, when the Yarra Bridge fell.

The giant, steel platform—which had been sitting 160 feet above the river—fell to the ground below, killing and injuring many of the workers.

A LADY NAMED AGNES

Agnes entered the Gulf of Mexico from the Caribbean and proceeded to threaten the coast of Florida. The hurricane did some damage to western Florida and then turned inland, over Alabama and Georgia. She seemed to loose speed, and there were good reasons to assume she would blow herself out. But the lady did a turnabout.

On June 21, a rejuvenated hurricane hit the southwestern tip of Virginia. Agnes poured tons of water on Virginia; Washington, D. C.; Maryland; Pennsylvania; New York; and New Jersey. Agnes had definitely not blown herself out.

If the Richmond state-guard engineers had not been able to rush heavy-capacity water purification machinery to the Virginia state capital, 250,000 residents of Richmond would have been totally without drinking water.

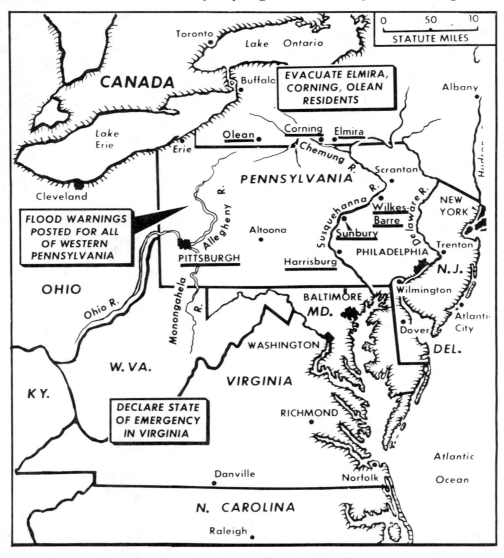

The areas which were hit hardest by hurricane Agnes covered a large section of the United States eastern seaboard. Evacuations took place in many localities, while others declared a state of emergency.

The girls in this rowboat were using the best possible means of street transportation in the flooded town of Mountain View, New Jersey.

The nation's capital suffered as Agnes approached the city of Washington. Bridges were out, and nearby suburbs had no water and no electricity. However, the storm continued on its way north without any more drastic damage there.

The hardest hit city in Maryland was Ellicott City, a community that was originally settled in 1772 as a mill community. Water power was needed for the mills. There was plenty of water during Agnes. Flood waters rose to the second-floor level of the houses on Main Street.

In Baltimore, Maryland, electricity was out, and low-lying areas were under water. Still, Agnes was not finished with the east coast.

In Pennsylvania, the Susquehanna River went crazy. Harrisburg's entire business district was under water. Even in the executive mansion of the Governor, water rose to touch the first-floor ceilings.

Houses, Farms, Bridges, and Entire Communities Under Water

The Schuylkill River overflowed its banks at Pottstown, Pennsylvania, and Pottstown was under water. From a helicopter, all that could be seen of the town were broken high tension wires and tops of tall trees. The candles people used for light could not be spotted from the air.

Owing Mills, Maryland, streets were washed out and major highways were impassable.

Main Street in Ellicott City, Maryland, stood under eight feet of water after the violent Agnes swept through.

Widespread damage from Agnes reached as far west as Pottstown, Pennsylvania—shown here under an estimated four feet of water.

The hardest hit town on Agnes' route was Wilkes-Barre, Pennsylvania. Here the dikes of the Susquehanna River gave way, and the river inundated the valley below, sweeping aside anything in its way. Houses, farms, bridges, and entire communities were under the water or floating on top. People were forced to climb onto the roofs of their houses to escape the rising water. Many rescue efforts were made in rowboats along what had once been streets.

Agnes continued her way into New York State. Here, she washed houses from their foundations and generally behaved in her own capricious manner, leaving debris in the communities she visited. The Corning Glass Works and Corning Museum suffered severe damage from the storm, and much irreplaceable Steuben glass was broken.

Still Agnes went on. She did not blow out to sea until she dropped water on parts of New Jersey and caused more flooding there.

In the wake of this hurricane, the property damage was almost astronomical. At least 25 cities were affected, and damage to crops was over $100 million. Whole commu-

nities were left without electricity, and over 5,000 businesses were destroyed. In view of the terrible destruction Agnes left behind her, it is almost a miracle that only 118 people lost their lives.

Hurricane Agnes had been carefully tracked by modern weather reporting, which gave advance warnings to affected areas. After Agnes hit, emergency efforts immediately began to send help to the stricken areas. People began to dig out and dry out from the effects of the hurricane.

In August, President Nixon, who had toured some of the flood areas, finally signed into law a Disaster Relief Supplemental Appropriation of nearly $1.6 billion. Added to what came from state, local, and private relief funds, this became the largest monetary outlay to help in a disaster up to that time.

There were hurricanes before Agnes and there have been many since. But for all who lived through the flooding in June of 1972, a lady named Agnes will be remembered as long as they live.

A FIRE ELEVEN STORIES OFF THE GROUND

190   February 1, 1974

People waited anxiously to be rescued by helicopter on the roof of the Joelma Building in downtown Sao Paulo, Brazil. A fire which broke out on the 11th floor was the cause for evacuation.

February is summertime in Brazil, and the summer of 1974 was very hot. As people went to work on February 1, they were already warm, and air conditioners were working at top speed.

Six hundred and fifty people poured into the tall Joelma Building in Sao Paulo to report for work. The building was 25 stories high, and its first 6 floors were parking facilities. Next came the offices of the Crefisul Bank;

above that bank were more offices.

Fire broke out on the eleventh floor of the building, probably in an over-heated air-conditioning vent. The fire spread very rapidly and moved in an upward course.

This picture shows the ambulances lined up at the burned-out bank building. The fire resulted in the deaths of over 200 people.

People below the fire line were able to escape—about 300 people on the lower floors made it safely to the street outside. The people above were not so fortunate. They were trapped by the quickly spreading smoke and flames.

The fire department lacked the equipment to cope with a fire in a skyscraper. Their ladders were too short and their hoses too weak to send water to the upper floors. The people trapped there had only two possibilities for escape—one was to jump from the windows to a possible death; the other was to climb to the roof to escape the heat and smoke and pray for rescue by air.

The fire was so hot that helicopters that had been called to the scene could only watch as victims ran around on the roof. The helicopters could not get close for two hours. When they were finally able to land, they found about 80 people burned and blackened but alive.

Four hours after it had begun, the terrible fire was controlled—but not before over 200 people had died and many more were injured.

In order to understand the fire at the Joelma Building, it is necessary to understand something about the city of Sao Paulo—population 8,000,000. In 1974, the city was the largest in Brazil and was still growing. Tall skyscrapers were constantly being built. Unfortunately, adequate fire regulations were not being enforced.

At the time of this fire, there were only 13 fire stations—each having about 100 firemen to serve the entire 8,000,000 people in Sao Paulo. Certainly, the lack of trained personnel was no help in controlling the fire, but there was also another fire-control problem confronting the city. Fires in skyscrapers must be fought differently from those in small buildings. They must be fought from inside rather than with ladders and hoses from the outside. The city fathers of Sao Paulo had not planned for this when the big building boom began.

With an inadequate fire department and an interior of plastic, paint, and wood, it is no surprise that the Joelma Building burned out of control for four hours. The sadness is that hindsight tells us that those who died in the fire might have been saved if more up-to-date fire-fighting methods had been used.

Investigators look into the rubble of the skyscraper. Inadequate fire fighting methods caused a tremendous loss of life.

TURKISH DC-10 CRASH NEAR PARIS

March 3, 1974

There were 117 passengers aboard the Turk Hava Yollari, a Turkish DC-10, from Istanbul to Paris. At Orly Airport, 217 others boarded the jet. With a crew of 12, the jumbo jet took off. The 346 people on board never made their destination to London.

The pilot did not radio that anything was wrong, but a few minutes before 1:00 p.m. the DC-10 fell from the sky, cutting a path approximately 3,000 feet long. Trees, parts of the plane, luggage, and bodies were strewn over a 9-mile area.

The crash was monitored by the French northern regional control center on their radar. The officers saw two blips on their screen. The moving blip was perhaps the aircraft. The stationary dot was items falling from the plane. This was later speculated to be the rear cargo door and two seats from the plane—with the occupants still strapped in by seat belts.

Firemen and rescue workers are shown surveying the remains of the Turkish Airlines jumbo jet. The plane crashed at Ermenonville, near Paris.

The unusual leaves on the trees were, in reality, the clothing of the crash victims.

The bodies of the dead were laid out in nearby fields. All 346 passengers aboard the jet were killed.

It took rescue teams more than three hours to reach the crash site at Ermenonville, near Paris. There was little they could do except begin the gruesome cleanup. Dawn of the next morning was just beginning to break when the first identifiable body was found.

Relatives waiting at Heathrow in London were told the awful truth. Feelings of fear, hope, horror, and disbelief ran through the crowd. A man fainted. A young woman attacked a member of the press. All wanted to know why.

First reports suggested that a terrorist bomb may have exploded on board the jet. This suggestion seemed plausible. Earlier that same day a band of rebels had forced a British DC-10 to touch down in Holland and had then burned it.

The true reason the plane crashed was far more disturbing, especially in view of the fact that it may have been totally avoidable. The cargo hatch cover was found seven miles from the plane. When this cover came off immediate decompression of the plane resulted.

The American team investigating the crash was aware of a similar problem in 1972. Then, an American Airlines DC-10 lost its cargo door. The rear floor of the cabin buckled. It was only because of the superb ability of the pilot that the plane was able to land safely. That DC-10 was found to have a faulty locking system. America's Federal Aviation Administration did nothing. The jet's manufacturer, McDonnell Douglas, merely requested that changes be made. Those requests were not mandatory. The Turkish DC-10 was built after those requests were issued. None of the necessary modifications had been made.

March 6, three days after the 346 people had died, the Federal Aviation Administration issued an order to all airlines that ran DC-10s. This order made all necessary changes mandatory. However, for the family and friends of the fallen Turkish airliner, that order was too little and far too late.

The international ramifications have resulted in a legal battle. It will hopefully resolve the question of the legal rights of airplane manufacturers, passengers, and plane operators. The insurance claims awarded to families of the passengers on that DC-10 were quite large. Perhaps this can ensure that future airplanes will fly with the assurance that known mechanical defects will be corrected.

The explosion at the Nypro Works near Flixborough, England, left 29 people dead, more than 100 injured, and 100 homes in the village either destroyed completely or badly damaged. The blast was heard 30 miles away.

The death toll at the chemical plant would have been far greater if the explosion and ensuing fire had occurred on a working day. As it was, on that Saturday afternoon a reduced staff of 70 was working where normally 550 people worked.

The blast, which occurred at 4:53 p.m., did much more than destroy the factory itself. Whole roofs of houses were lifted off like cardboard in the town of Flixborough. Doors were wrenched off their hinges, and windows smashed into splinters. Even people were picked up and tossed around—some never to be recovered because of the tremendous force of the blast and the fire that followed.

Flixborough, England was the location of the Nypro Works—a chemical plant which was ruined by an explosion. The explosion destroyed 100 homes in the village as well.

As far as 1½ miles away, glass splintered from the force of the explosion even before the noise was heard. Two little girls playing outside had to be rushed to the hospital—with glass splinters in their faces.

Witnesses as far as 6 miles away described the blast as looking like an atom bomb, complete to a mushroom cloud. Others declared that the explosion was as awful as any wartime bombing. The ensuing fire burned for 24 hours, destroying everything within the factory and leaving behind nothing but a burned-out metal frame.

The plant was jointly owned by the British National Coal Board and the Dutch State Mining Company. It was here that a vital ingredient for nylon was being made—by name, caprolactam. This was essential in the making of nylon products and was being turned out by the chemical plant at the rate of 20,000 tons a year. It was shipped all over the world to be used in the manufacture of everything from nylon underwear to automobile tires.

Explosion Caused By A Leak In A Gas Pipe

In 1973, the Flixborough plant began to use a shortcut in the manufacture of caprolactam. Instead of using cyclohexane, they switched to the highly toxic explosive, benzene. Chemical changes under great pressure created the caprolactam, which in turn was changed into the nylon products the world now demanded.

The explosion on that June Saturday was caused by a leak in a gas pipe. The effect on the world manufacture of nylon products was drastic, since the plant at Flixborough supplied the world with most of its caprolactam.

Witnesses from as far as six miles away described the explosion as looking like an atom bomb, complete with a mushroom cloud. This is how the Nypro Works looked from the air.

After the explosion and total destruction of the plant, the world had to reconsider how good or harmful the giant industrial monopolies actually were.

Public reaction from people in and around Flixborough was shock. They were not aware of the danger hidden in their own backyards by the walls of the Nypro Works.

As a result of this explosion at Flixborough, future industrialists would consider the potential danger of their plants to the surrounding areas. Two types of problems were brought clearly into focus. The first was the leakage of volatile liquids or gases that can explode. The second was the sudden release of toxic material that, if escaping

The roof of this house in the village of Flixborough was ripped off from the force of the blast.

Huge columns of smoke and flame continued to burn for hours after the actual explosion had occurred.

into the air, could cause casualties many miles beyond the point of release.

The explosion at the Nypro plant destroyed not only the plant itself, but also the small rural community of Flixborough—population 300 people. No home was without damage from the explosion. Ironically, not one of the residents of Flixborough worked at the plant.

Firemen were unable to control the blaze until the day after the original blast.

Although the Nypro Works was devastated by the explosion on Saturday, the death toll would have been far greater had the explosion and ensuing fire occurred on a regular working day.

CAUSE OF THE CRASH-UNKNOWN

Eastern Airlines Boeing 727 Flight 66 was arriving late from New Orleans, but it was only a few minutes after its estimated time of arrival, and neither the jetliner's pilot nor those in the control tower at Kennedy Airport in New York were concerned. Conditions at Kennedy were wet and rainy but not too bad for flights to land.

Two earlier flights that had arrived at Kennedy had been aware of what pilots call wind shear. This is a hard-to-detect condition of turbulence that can actually suck a plane down. Wind shear is caused by opposite directions of two violent air currents meeting in a vortex and creating the power to suck up anything that comes in its way.

Although these reports were given to the control tower, the instruments there showed nothing unusual. Besides, both of the reporting planes had landed with no real problems.

Eastern Airlines' flight 66 crashed at the edge of Rockaway Boulevard, near Kennedy Airport in New York City. The death toll reached 112.

Policemen view the wreckage of the Eastern Airlines' jetliner as DC-8 prepares to land at Kennedy.

These were the conditions when Flight 66 reported and requested permission to land. The tower gave the needed permission but did warn of the possibility of wind shear as well as the fact that the approach end of the runway was wet. Eastern Flight 66 did not answer the control tower.

Rockaway Boulevard, a main artery between New York and Long Island, was just beginning to fill up with

Firemen and rescue workers move through the plane's debris. The fallen approach light tower is in the background.

Bodies of the victims lay underneath shrouds, as a priest kneels to administer the last rites of the church.

homeward-bound commuters. At 4 p.m. it was not as crowded as it would be later, but there were still many long lines of cars making their way out of New York City.

None of those people riding on the expressway were concerned when they heard a jetliner overhead. They were close enough to Kennedy Airport that this was a common occurrence. However, when what seemed to be a flash of lightning occurred and an immediate crash fol-

lowed, the people in nearby cars were very well aware that something terrible had happened.

The crash of the huge jet sent burning wreckage all over the road. Cars had to brake frantically to avoid the wreckage as well as other cars, all trying to cope with wet streets, burning airplane pieces, and oil- and fuel-covered roadways. People on the ground who witnessed this felt the terrible shock that raw death always brings forth. Not many of the airliner's passengers lived to think at all.

When the jet crashed, 116 people were on board; 110 died immediately. Of those who managed to get out of the burning aircraft, 2 more died of burns in the hospital. Rockaway Boulevard was turned into a morgue in a matter of minutes.

Police and firemen converged at the scene of the wreck. Although the firemen were wearing asbestos suits, the fire moved more swiftly than they did. It took only a short time to smother the burning wreck with foam, but it was too late for most of the people in the plane. Only 14 people were taken alive to nearby hospitals.

Human remains were laid on the side of the road and covered with white sheets. The heavy rain beat down on the sheets, showing that there were young children as well as adults there on the roadside. Even an infant's body was found, one which had not been listed on the passenger manifesto.

The investigation that followed the crash of the Boeing 727 was not definitive as to the cause. Since it is an unusual occurrence for lightning to do grave damage to an airplane, this was probably not the cause. Did an unseen wind shear draw the big plane into it, causing the crash? The question could not be answered. Did the pilot misjudge where he was? Since the pilot died in the crash, there was no way of knowing this, either.

The questions raised by the crash of Eastern's Flight 66 will never be answered. All we know for sure is that the crash carried 112 people to their deaths, leaving behind grieving relatives and many questions that will never be answered.

Rockaway Boulevard, where this aerial photograph was taken, was turned into a morgue in a matter of minutes.

8.2 ON THE RICHTER SCALE

204   July 28, 1976

The Hopei Province of China borders the Gulf of Po Hai and includes the capital city of Peking, Tienstin, and what was once Tangshan. The earthquake that totaled the city of Tangshan measured 8.2 on the Richter scale.

Tangshan, a coal and steel city of one million inhabitants, produced rail locomotives, diesel engines, and other heavy machinery needed in China's Five Year Plan. In addition, Tangshan was China's largest single producer of coal. It was a very productive, busy place before the earthquake of July 28, 1976.

At 3:40 a.m. on the morning of July 28, Tangshan was totally destroyed. There was no apparent warning before this earthquake, despite the fact that China had an elaborate system for predicting earthquakes. Scientific information is gathered at 5,000 separate locations and fed into fully equipped seismographic centers. This time, the system did not work.

In the Hopei Province of China, people took refuge outdoors after the powerful earthquake made their houses into death traps.

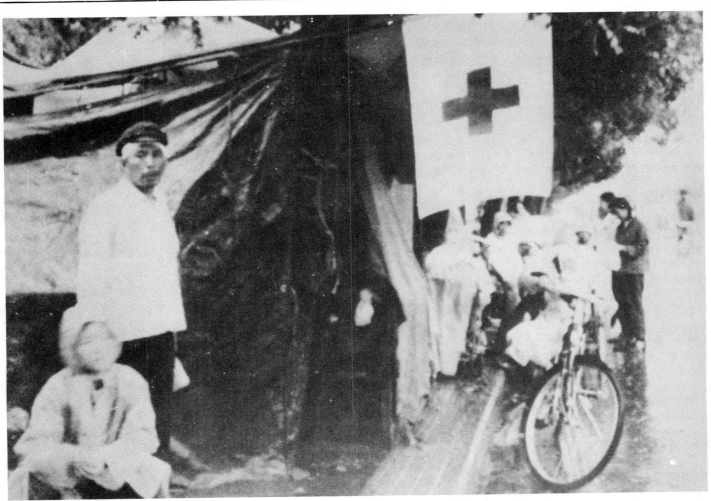

Peking residents waited their turns at an emergency first aid station. This facility was set up downtown after heavy damage and casualties were reported in the city.

Doctors examined victims in Tangshan, a city of one million people which was totally destroyed.

The young girl shown here made her home in a drainpipe. Other people salvaged what they could from their demolished houses and took shelter wherever they could find it.

The massive tremor and the aftershock, which followed 16 hours later, killed more than 100,000 people. Those who survived had terrible stories to tell about whole walls falling and whole buildings crashing into piles of debris.

The port city of Tienstin, 60 miles from Tangshan, felt effects of the quake. The Tienstin Friendship Guest House stood 9 stories high. The building was literally cut in half and separated from itself by a gap about 12 inches wide.

Peking was 100 miles from Tangshan, the "epicenter" of the earthquake. As a result of this distance, the capital city did not suffer extreme damage, although some of its older buildings did fall.

Typical of the size of this disaster is the following quote:

"Only about 50 people in the capital were killed by the initial shock." [After the hundreds of thousands who died at Tangshan, 50 seemed very few.]

Although there had been no warning earth tremors before the quake, Chinese authorities responded quickly to the needs of their stricken people. Trucks loaded with everything from prefabricated houses to shovels to dig out the dead and dying were immediately started on their way to Tangshan. Recovery from the earthquake was begun, but it would be a long time, if ever, before things were as they once had been.

A slightly ironic postscript for earthquake-detection in an era of scientific data can be found in a 1973 pamphlet from the Earthquake Office in Tienstin. It reads in part that an earthquake may be imminent:

"When cattle, sheep or horses refuse to get into the corral,

When rats run out from their hiding place,

When chickens fly up to the trees and pigs break out from their pens,

When ducks refuse to go to the water and dogs bark for no obvious reason . . . .

When fish jump out of the water as if frightened."

Even the warnings listed in this pamphlet for the Chinese peasants did not prepare anyone for the earthquake at Tangshan.

Nearly one year after the earthquake, the effects were still visible. This picture, taken many months later, shows a damaged building near the Tangshan train station.

Suitcases and personal effects, such as a woman's wig, scattered over the ground at the fogged-in Los Rodeos Airport after a horrible two-plane crash.

The scene for this unbelievable disaster is the Canary Islands—just off the west coast of Africa. This is where many Europeans normally end their search for the sun; it was and is a popular vacation spot. The early spring of 1977 was no exception. Visitors were coming and going to the Islands in droves.

The main airport for the entire group of Islands was located at Las Palmas on Grand Canary Island. It was at Las Palmas that a terrorist bomb caused some minor damage and a few injuries. A florist shop was destroyed and at least five people were injured. This unrest combined with terrorist threats caused the Spanish authorities to divert incoming planes to safety at Los Rodeos Airport at Santa Cruz on Tenerife Island.

The Los Rodeos Airport was jammed with airplanes on that Sunday afternoon of March 27. In addition to the coming and going of many planes, a fog was making conditions on the ground continuously worse. Los Rodeos did not have ground radar and so could not track runway traffic that way. The three air-traffic controllers had to depend on what they could see and on radio reports. The foggy afternoon made vision very limited.

KLM's flight 4805 was due to continue its journey from the Canary Islands at 5 p.m. The fire-blackened wreckage shown was all that was left of the great plane after the crash.

At 1:44 p.m., KLM flight 4805 arrived at Los Rodeos from Amsterdam with 248 aboard. The big Dutch jet was directed to park at the far end of the runway. The pilot was Captain Jacob Veldhuizen Van Zantem, a 51-year-old man with much flying experience. Flight 4805 was scheduled to continue on its way later that afternoon.

Captain Victor Grubbs was piloting the Pan Am flight 1736 from Los Angeles and New York. This plane arrived at Los Rodeos at 3 p.m. with 378 passengers and 16 crew members. This plane was also directed to park at the far end of the runway.

At 5 p.m., the runway was extremely foggy—pilots could not see more than 1,600 feet ahead. There was a backup of 11 aircraft, including the two jumbo jets, waiting for takeoff instructions.

The air-traffic controller's plan was to hold the KLM until after the Pan Am was reported clear of the runway. No one realized that both jets were on the same runway.

No one knows how the misunderstanding occurred. Perhaps the Dutch captain did not hear the tower instruction to stand by. Undoubtedly, he did not know that the Pan Am flight had not left the runway.

The two planes started for takeoff at opposite points of the runway. Although both pilots made desperate efforts to clear each other. There was not enough time or space to do this.

The KLM crashed into the Pan Am at midship as the Pan Am pilot swerved to the left. The top of the Pan Am jet was cut off immediately, causing a fire in the first-class lounge. The KLM bounced off the contact along the runway and exploded about 500 yards away—instantly killing all 248 people on board.

Over 300 people died on the Pan Am jumbo; about 64 more were injured. The total dead from both planes numbered 580. The runway at Los Rodeos was covered with broken fragments of the two airplanes, personal belongings of the passengers, and assorted other rubble and debris. It was a horrible sight.

Investigations of the crash did not discover anything more than has already been told. The Dutch pilot was killed in his KLM and so could not answer as to what he had or had not heard from the tower on that terrible Sunday afternoon.

The three countries, involved—Spain, the Netherlands, and the United States—all held investigations, but nothing could be proved. Lawsuits by survivors and families of the dead were held, and settlements, both in and out of court, reached hundreds of millions of dollars.

Of all known facts, perhaps the saddest is that this terrible crash of two jumbo jetliners happened on the ground. A foggy, misty Sunday afternoon in a small airport without ground radar brought about the unexpected for 580 people whose holiday trips ended in death.

Scattered wreckage of both planes could be seen from the airport's control tower after the fog lifted.

This was the scene on the runway of Los Rodeos Airport.

Bodies of unidentified victims were lined up in concrete vaults for a mass memorial service in Westminster, California. The collision resulted in the death of 580 people.

THE BURNING OF A SUPPER CLUB

The headline performer on that Saturday night of Memorial Day weekend was singer John Davidson. There were 600 people crowded into the Cabaret Room of the Beverly Hills Supper Club ready to enjoy the show. The other rooms of the club were also full, and the total number of people in the club was more than 3,000. Everyone was in a festive mood as the food and drinks were passed.

Many People Came Across The River

The Beverly Hills Supper Club had been an illegal gambling house in the 1950s. By the 1970s, it was a popular supper club set on a hill in Southgate, Kentucky, beside the Ohio River. Cincinnati was on the other side of the river, and certainly many people came across the river to the popular club.

Fire Began In The Walls

In addition to the well-known Cabaret Room, the club had many private rooms and other smaller dining areas for their patrons. Such picturesque names as the Zebra room, the Venetian rooms, Garden rooms, and the Wedding Chapel were on the doors of the smaller sections of the club.

From this 1972 picture, the plush and elegant interior of the Beverly Hills Supper Club was ready for patrons. The club had been rebuilt after a fire in 1970.

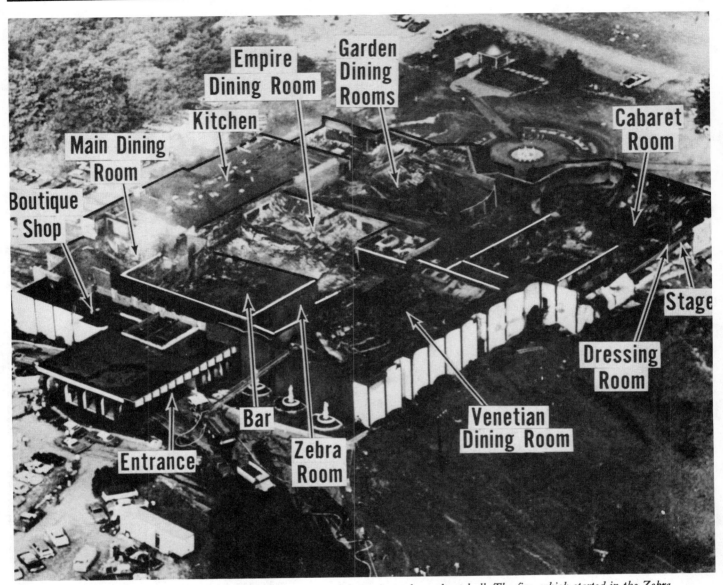

On the day after the fire on Memorial Day weekend, the supper club was just a burned-out hull. The fire, which started in the Zebra Room quickly spread throughout the rest of the club.

Fire was the last thing on the minds of the festive patrons that night. There had been a fire at the club in the early 1970s, but no one had been hurt and the fire was quickly controlled.

Members of a wedding party in the Zebra Room of the Supper Club complained of being hot. Fire experts later ascertained that the fire had actually begun in the walls of the Zebra Room. By the time the departing wedding party complained of the heat, the fire had probably been smoldering for an hour. The time was about 8:45 p.m.

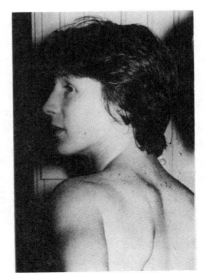

Busboy Walter Bailey, age 16, interruped the show on the stage of the Cabaret Room and pointed out the fire exits to the audience. He helped lead many groups of patrons to safety.

The morning after the fire, firemen had to check through what remained of the once-fashionable supper club. They discovered that a short circuit in the club's electrical system had caused the fire.

Employees ran for fire extinguishers and tried to control the fire. Three fire extinguishers were not enough to put out the blaze. Flames quickly reached up to the ceiling of the room, and black smoke began to filter through the ventilators and air-conditioning system. No fire alarm was sent to the fire department.

In the Cabaret Room, a 16-year-old busboy kept his wits about him. Walter Bailey interrupted the comedy act on stage by stepping to the microphone.

"There's a small fire," he said. "Everyone stay calm and please exit the building."

People did begin to file out in an orderly way. However, the fire and smoke increased in intensity. Still no

alarm had been sent to the fire department.

At 9:01 p.m. the first alarm was turned in, 21 minutes after the fire had been spotted. Would an immediate alarm have saved some of the lives that were lost? It might at least have helped.

A short circuit in the club's electrical system, caused by the fire, plunged the club into darkness. Panic took over as people stampeded to escape the smoke and flames. Although there were actually nine exits from the club, only a small number of people had direct access to the outside. Most had to make their way through dark, smoke-filled corridors to escape.

When the first fire trucks arrived, there was little they

could do. There was so much black, gaseous smoke and such high heat from fire that the firemen could not get inside to help those who were trapped. People were later found in weird positions along the walls where they had died. Some were still seated at their tables. They had not had time to get up and try to escape before they perished from smoke inhalation.

There were 1,500 cars parked in the club parking lot at the time of the fire. Police later checked license plates to identify those who died in the fire on that holiday night.

The final figure from the Beverly Hills Supper Club fire was 161 dead. At least 129 more were injured from burns or smoke inhalation. The statistics of this fire were not quite as bad as those from the Cocoanut Grove fire in Boston—but panic as well as fire helped to claim bodies for the morgues.

Rescue workers struggled well into the next day to free bodies of victims. The ruins of the building yielded so many bodies that in some places they were stacked three feet high. A volunteer described the aftermath of the fire, saying:

"Their flesh is welded to the steel beams."

Could the fire at the Beverly Hills Supper Club have been avoided? The club had no automatic sprinkler system that might have made this a minor fire. Such a system would have automatically notified the fire department, saved at least 20 minutes and many lives.

The horror of a fire in a public building once again combined with panic and brought awful results. Unfortunately, there is no way of guaranteeing that this will be the last fire of its kind. As sad as it may seem, it could happen again.

FLOODING AT TOCCOA FALLS

216   November 6, 1977

The Toccoa Falls Bible School was built in 1907 by educator Richard A. Forrest. It sat in a quiet valley in Georgia and was named after the creek and falls which flowed nearby.

In 1942, as the school increased in size, it needed more water and power. To provide this, Mr. R.G. Le Tourneau, a philanthropist with deep interest in the school, had an earthen embankment built about a half mile above the falls. This resulted in a dam and a lake which ran 35 feet deep near the school.

Toccoa Creek, which ran in a winding course on the school campus, was gentle. In fact, the 80-acre lake below the dam was used for recreation. Since the school used other sources of power from 1954 on, no one bothered about either the lake or the stream—except to enjoy them both.

When Toccoa Creek flooded, the Toccoa Falls Bible School was not the only property to suffer much damage; the huge waves which swept downstream also destroyed a nearby trailer park. The trailers shown here look like children's toys after the effects of the flood.

Rescue workers, including some students from the Bible School, are shown carrying a victim of the flood waters.

The Bible School continued to grow, and more buildings were erected to hold its students and staff—some of those buildings on the banks of the stream. A nearby trailer park called Trailer Village had 25 trailers all situated in the picturesque setting. The last building to be erected at the school was a four-story brick dormitory called Forrest Hall after the Bible School's founder.

Rain poured down on the Bible School for three days in early November. By November 5, there was so much rain that power was cut off for four hours, coming back on at 11 p.m. By 12 a.m., all was quiet on campus, and 425 students and 175 staff members were sound asleep. But Toccoa Creek was swollen from all the rain—and a maintenance man and two volunteer firemen were keeping an eye out for trouble.

Trouble arrived at 1:30 a.m. on November 6, when huge waves swept down on the three men. They were unable to alert the sleeping campus of the Bible School.

Although the maintenance man was able to save himself from the rushing water, the two volunteer firemen drowned.

The force of the wall of water from the broken dam was such that it carried huge boulders, trees, and debris along with it. Houses were smashed apart and trailers from Trailer Village were lifted up and carried away. The new Forrest Hall building did remain standing, although all of its first-floor windows were smashed by the racing water. Forrest Hall was flooded to the ceilings on the first floor in a matter of seconds.

The damage occurred in just 30 minutes, but, by the end of that awful half hour, 39 persons were dead. Dozens more were injured—all of the victims belonging to the Bible School as either students, faculty, or staff.

When the water had finished its devastation, those who lived eagerly began to cleanup. Although all mourned those victims which the flood had claimed, there seemed to be a renewed faith in God. The president of the school announced that it would be closed for only a few days—reopening for classes on November 15.

The collapse of the 40-year-old dam at Toccoa Falls

The search for flood victims was a grim job for the firemen who came from nearby counties to help.

once again focused the nation's attention on the thousands of private dams all over the country. The nation learned from legislators that the 1972 Federal Dam Inspection Act had accomplished little due to lack of funds.

Although efforts were indeed made after the collapse of the dam at Toccoa Falls, there is still danger from dams which need repairs or reinforcement in order to be protected from floods.

Representative Leo J. Ryan of California summed up the dam situation thusly:

"These dams are a loaded shotgun pointed at the people downstream."

This was certainly true at Toccoa Falls.

These students from the Bible School survey what was left after a wall of water carried huge boulders, trees, and other debris along its path.

The awful damage pictured here occurred in just 30 minutes. At the end of that time, 39 persons were dead and dozens more were injured.

MASSACRE AT GUYANA

November 18, 1978

A religious cult headed by Jim Jones was known as the People's Temple. Originally, the People's Temple was located in San Francisco—and when Jim Jones spoke, people came to listen by the thousands. There was a mesmerizing quality to the tone of Jones' voice, and, like other fanatical leaders, he had a way of convincing others he was right.

Commune Turns Into Nightmare

By 1977, San Francisco was no longer the home base of the People's Temple. Jim Jones purchased land from the government of Guyana and moved his people down to the jungle commune which he called Jonestown. Located 150 miles northwest of Guyana's capital city, Georgetown, the commune looked like any other happy community in a jungle setting.

However, citizens in the United States were questioning what was happening at Jonestown. Stories were coming to light of beatings, brainwashing, labor forced at gunpoint, and imprisonment of people. Representative Leo Ryan, a 53-year-old Democrat from California, went to investigate the Jonestown rumors.

This land purchased by Jim Jones in Guyana housed the headquarters of Jones' religious cult called the "People's Temple."

Representative Leo Ryan, a Democrat from California, was ambushed and shot just before he was to board a plane and return to the United States. The congressman was there to investigate Jones' activities at the commune.

The dead bodies lying on the steps of the pavillion of the People's Temple are the result of a mass suicide.

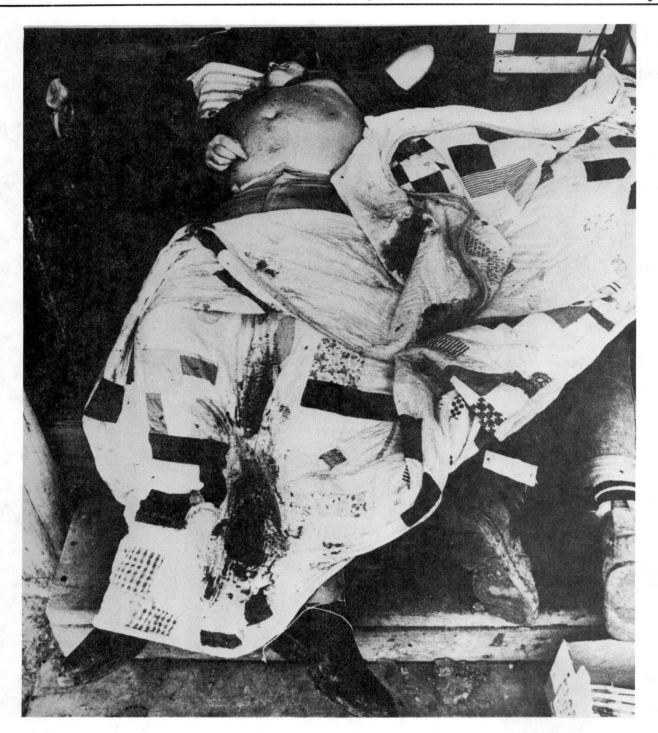

Reverend Jim Jones, who ordered the suicide, was found about five feet from his jungle throne. This picture was taken two days after Jones' death.

Ryan, with a group of 18 people—including some members of the press—flew to Guyana. On the day of his arrival, all seemed to go well. Ryan was shown around the commune by a gracious Jim Jones. The next day, November 18, Ryan began asking some questions.

The congressman was attacked with a hunting knife by a Jones lieutenant and immediately decided to leave. His party, along with 16 people who chose to defect from Jonestown, went by truck to the Port Kaituma airstrip eight miles away. Before anyone could board the plane, shooting broke out which killed Ryan and four other Americans and wounded ten other people. A television cameraman kept filming until a bullet stopped him. The films from his camera told a horrible story to a horrified world. No one realized that this was only the beginning of a greater unbelievable horror yet to come.

When Jim Jones was told of the murders on the airstrip on November 19, he ordered all of his people to a

This "vat of death" was where the suicide drink was mixed. Those who died drank a mixture consisting of flavored soft drink, potassium cyanide, and an assortment of painkillers.

For those too young to drink poison from a cup, the poison was sprayed down their throats with hypodermic syringes. Some of the empty cups and syringes are shown here.

mass meeting at the open-air pavillion. The faithful were surrounded by armed guards. The time had arrived, according to Jones, to enact in reality a suicide pact which had been practiced many times before.

The suicide drink was a flavored soft drink which had potassium cyanide and an assortment of painkillers in it. It was prepared in huge vats and dispensed in cups. For those too young to drink from a cup, the poison was sprayed down their throats by a syringe.

Over 900 people—some voluntarily, others at gunpoint—drank the poisoned brew and died within five minutes. Babies and young children died in their parents' arms and families laid down together, faces buried in the dirt, to await their deaths. Death was not long in coming. Jones himself died of a gunshot wound in his head.

The aftermath of the carnage was grotesque. The bodies which laid all over the compound in the jungle heat produced a sickening stench. The work of identification and placement of the bodies in coffins was a mammouth task. The United States sent in Army transport planes to carry the dead home for burial.

Television cameras were on the scene as well as other members of the press. The pictures which came back to the United States were shocking—the story of how it all came about even more so. The public at large now realized what only a few worried families had known—that Jim Jones was a religious fanatic who ordered the death of over 900 of his followers.

The mass suicide proved to be the end of the People's Temple.

THE DISASTER THAT ALMOST WAS

March 28, 1979   225

The four cooling towers at the nuclear energy plant at Three Mile Island stood 372 feet high. Two high-domed nuclear reactor containers were on the site which was located 11 miles southeast of Harrisburg, Pennsylvania. The nuclear plant belonged to the Metropolitan Edison Company and generated 880 megawatts of electricity from the huge turbines at Unit 2.

At 4 a.m. on March 28, Unit 2 shut off automatically and alarm sirens alerted the men working that shift. The few technicians there had no way of knowing that this alarm would be any more serious than earlier bugs which had been easily corrected. Before many hours had passed, the story was changed. An entire community was threatened, and thousands of people were evacuated from the immediate area.

The danger on Three Mile Island was from the possibility of a "meltdown." This could occur if the nuclear core were to drop into the water coolant at the bottom of the chamber, in turn causing a steam explosion. The possible explosion could break the four foot thick concrete walls of the container and release deadly radioactive gas into the atmosphere. It could have been a nuclear holocaust.

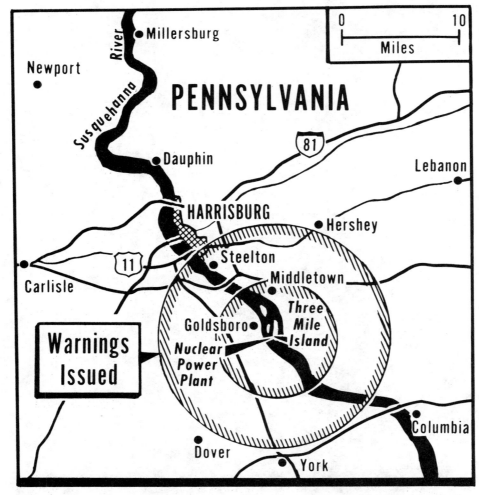

This map shows the area which was evacuated by order of Governor Dick Thornburgh of Pennsylvania. The danger of a "meltdown" from the nuclear plant at Three Mile Island had been the basis of the Governor's decision.

The Three Mile Island Nuclear Generating Plant looks like this from the air. To the right is where the incident occurred.

This church, located near the leaking power plant, had almost no attendance on Sunday. The reverend did preach a sermon for the four ladies who attended.

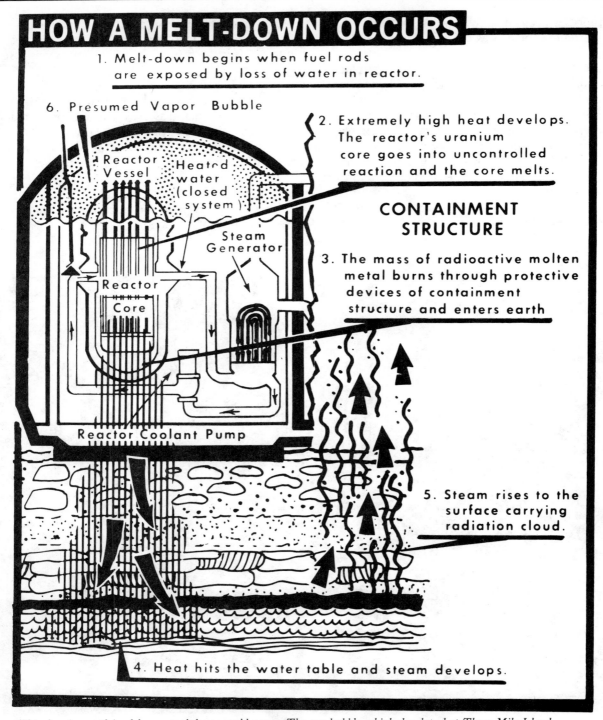

HOW A MELT-DOWN OCCURS

1. Melt-down begins when fuel rods are exposed by loss of water in reactor.

6. Presumed Vapor Bubble

Reactor Vessel

Heated water (closed system)

2. Extremely high heat develops. The reactor's uranium core goes into uncontrolled reaction and the core melts.

CONTAINMENT STRUCTURE

Steam Generator

Reactor Core

3. The mass of radioactive molten metal burns through protective devices of containment structure and enters earth

Reactor Coolant Pump

5. Steam rises to the surface carrying radiation cloud.

4. Heat hits the water table and steam develops.

This drawing explained how a meltdown could occur. The gas bubble which developed at Three Mile Island threatened thousands of nearby residents, including those in the city of Harrisburg.

The day the nightmare began was a Wednesday. Thursday brought forth reassuring reports from the public relations man at Metropolitan Edison. The National Regulatory Commission (NRC) at King of Prussia, Pennsylvania, was not so sure. Their report showed detection of radioactivity 16 miles from the plant. Members of the press began to assemble to put out the latest word on what was growing to be the biggest story of the year.

By Friday morning, the world's attention was focused on Three Mile Island. Pennsylvania's Governor Richard Thornburgh issued a warning to those within a ten-mile radius to remain indoors with their windows shut. He also ordered the closing of schools within a five-mile radius. The evacuation of pregnant women and young children began.

The governor also closed the Harrisburg airport and warned all Harrisburg citizens to prepare for evacuation should authorities deem it necessary. A gas bubble had developed in the reactor. It was possible that a meltdown would begin.

The scientists and engineers worked around the clock, while the world watched and waited. President Carter sent the NRC's chief operations officer to take complete charge at Three Mile Island. The Defense Department was busy preparing in the event Governor Thornburgh ordered a mass evacuation. On Sunday, President Carter visited the crippled plant. Curfews were imposed on near-by towns, and the Red Cross was prepared to move on an instant's notice.

This story does not have an ending, although there was no nuclear explosion and no mass evacuation. The gas bubble in the reactor was controlled, and life on the banks of the Susquehanna River in Pennsylvania got back to normal. But the future of nuclear plants was a source of great controversy.

Is There a Future For Nuclear Plants?

People with placards picketed and protested nuclear plants as being environmentally unsafe. The scientists and engineers are still looking for better ways to implement nuclear energy and at the same time protect people in nearby communities.

The fate of future nuclear plants still hangs in the balance, as a result of the nuclear incident which took place at Three Mile Island.

Signs protesting against nuclear energy were posted along the deserted street of Goldsboro, Pennsylvania. Most of the people in the town had voluntarily evacuated the area.

With their seat belts securely fastened, the 258 passengers and 14 crew members on American Airlines' flight 191 prepared for takeoff. The time was 3 p.m. on a clear, sunny Friday afternoon and the place was Chicago's O'Hare Airport. The flight was to be a four hour non-stop one to Los Angeles. However, not one passenger or crew member reached their destination.

The fated plane had arrived at the Chicago airport a few hours before the scheduled 3 p.m. flight. Captain Walter H. Lux was piloting the jumbo jet. As the plane lifted off, the controller in the tower realized that something was wrong. He radioed Captain Lux and asked whether he'd wanted to come back. There was no time for the captain to reply.

In a matter of seconds, the left turbofan engine of the great airplane had broken loose of its moorings. The engine fell off onto the runway and fuel was pouring out of the hole where the engine should have been.

This McDonnell Douglas DC-10, photographed in 1970, was the same kind of plane as the American Airlines DC-10 which crashed to the ground at O'Hare Airport.

The jet climbed a few hundred feet before it turned perpendicular to the ground and fell in an abandoned airfield near a trailer park in Elk Grove Village. The explosion of the plane allowed no chance of survival for any of the passengers or crew.

Flames from the wreckage were seen as far away as eight miles and at least one home in the trailer park burned up as well. Had the plane not disintegrated as quickly as it did, more damage to the mobile homes would have occurred.

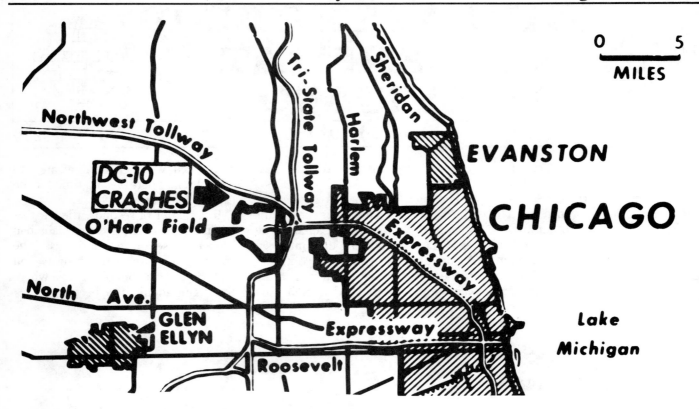

The airplane, which was en route to Los Angeles, climbed to an altitude of a few hundred feet before it fell and crashed into an abandoned airfield near a Trailer Park in Elk Grove Village.

Although firemen battled the blaze, the explosion of the plane allowed no chance of survival for any of the passengers or crew.

Litter covered the runway after the DC-10 crash. The forklift truck in the background removed the engine which fell from the aircraft onto the runway.

The flames were so intense that rescue workers could not get near the wreckage for an hour. When they could finally move in, all that remained for them to do was the ghoulish task of marking the charred bodies and uniden-tified remains. Colored markers on wooden stakes dotted the field to show were bodies lay among all that remained of the DC-10.

Rescue workers shown here were marking the charred bodies and unidentified remains of the crash victims.

The National Transportation Safety Board sent a team to investigate the crash—which was not the first one of a McDonnell Douglas DC-10. As a result of the crash and the investigation which followed, all DC-10s were grounded in the United States and declared unsafe to fly. But that was after the fact. Nothing could change the tragedy which occurred at O'Hare Airport at the start of that Memorial Day weekend.

These two victims, found in the streets of Morvi, were among many thousands who died when heavy rains caused the Manchu River Dam to collapse.

Heavy rains and winds were nothing new to the people of India. Monsoons were a common and seasonal occurrence. Since most people were used to this phenomenon of nature, they were adequately prepared. Then, the unexpected happened—a dam broke and the death toll was in the thousands.

Morvi, an industrial city consisting of approximately 70,000 people, was located 300 miles northwest of Bombay in the state of Gujarat. Its primary industry was pottery and ceramics, and the revenues generated from these factories helped to make Morvi an attractive city. There were many parks where mothers brought children to play and couples in love went to stroll. Wide, broad streets led to homes of mud and concrete, schools, and factories.

Six miles north of Morvi stood the Manchu River Dam. Built in 1972, it was 197 feet high. The engineers had built it to withstand an average yearly rainfall of 22 inches and a water pressure of 200,000 cubic feet per second. It protected Morvi and 30 small villages between that city and the Manchu River.

Since the end of July, Morvi had been experiencing heavy monsoon rains. Then, a storm dropped 28 inches of rain on Morvi in less than 24 hours.

As the unsuspecting townspeople went about their daily chores on August 11, engineers tried frantically to relieve the increasing water pressure of the dam. Water levels rose 20 feet above normal and the pressure within the dam had doubled. The engineers tried in vain to open the sluice gates. Rust, accumulated from lack of use, failed to save a town.

Without warning, the dam broke. A 20-foot wall of water raced from the dam; within 15 minutes, everything in its path lay devastated. Mothers watched helplessly as children were swept away by the angry waters, unable to answer their cries for help. Entire families were gone. Mud homes were completely destroyed. Brick and concrete buildings were devastated. Slimy mud reached to the second story of many of the buildings that were left standing. Layers of mud covered everything else.

Some estimates say that four feet of mud covered the streets. Bodies lay everywhere. As one observer quoted:

"Wherever you put your foot in the mud, you strike a body."

This cow was caught on the eaves of a building and left hanging there when the waters finally receded.

This young boy in Morvi was pinned to the wall by raging flood waters—another victim among the thousands who lost their lives.

Some estimates said that four feet of mud covered the streets of Morvi. Bodies were everywhere, as this picture shows.

Tens of thousands were left homeless and without available food or water. As all communication sources had been destroyed, news of the disaster was delayed for more than 12 hours.

The rescue efforts that were finally begun were hampered by continued rain, wind, and mud. The roads were covered with debris and bodies. The elements made air relief almost impossible. Railroad tracks were gone. Some people claimed later that the poorly-manned rescue effort was the fault of the ruling political party. For whatever the reason, the statistics are unbelievable.

By the end of the day on August 12, 25,000 food packets were finally delivered to the survivors. Most of them had been without any nourishment for the preceding 24 hours.

Initial damage to factories, homes, and buildings was estimated at $10 million. Sixty percent of all the buildings were either totally destroyed or damaged beyond use. Thirty-thousand townspeople left Morvi for refugee camps or the homes of relatives in other towns.

The greatest tragedy, the loss of life, is difficult to estimate. In the town of Morvi alone, the count was approximately 15,000. The number of dead in the 30 villages stretching between Morvi and the dam is not known as the area was completely cut off from relief efforts.

Some things cannot be measured in dollars. Broken families can never be reunited. Nature cannot be altered. However, the question as to why sluice gates, which could have averted the tragedy, did not work has yet to be disclosed. The town of Morvi slowly rebuilds while it waits agonizingly for that answer.

England was experiencing an unusually warm summer, and beaches were crowded with vacationers enjoying the calm seas. At least 306 yachts from 20 countries gathered at the Isle of Wight for the annual British racing classic—the Fastnet. Sailors have flocked to this small English town since 1925 to test their seafaring abilities from Cowes on the Isle of Wight to Fastnet Rock in southern Ireland and back to Plymouth, England. In doing so, they would have to navigate both the English Channel and the Atlantic Ocean. The entire trip was 605 miles long.

Several Fastnet races had been unchallenging for men of the sea. Competition had been dull and thoughts returned to the race of 1957 and the gale of that year: forty-one yachts entered that Fastnet but only 12 finished. The crew of that year's winner, America's *Carina II*, had to manually pump out the water which flooded in through a cracked hull. In the preceding 27 races, there was only one fatality when a middle-aged sailor suffered a heart attack in 1977. The 1979 Fastnet would prove to be vastly different.

On August 11, weather reports forecasted winds from 39 to 46 miles per hour, with even calmer winds at the race's farthest point. Excitement and tension increased as the boats took to the water. This year, a newer, lighter boat—called a ''light-displacement racing yacht''—was to be put to the test.

The French Admiral's Cup entrant Accanito, shown here during an earlier race, suffered damage in the high gales and mountainous seas during the Fastnet Race of 1979.

The Ariadne, also entered in the race, was reported to have sunk. Two of its crew members were dead and three others were rescued. Here, the yacht is shown with its mast broken before it sank in the high waves.

The Royal Navy rescue station at Culdrose in Cornwall sent helicopters to aid in the rescue of crewmen on the competing yachts. This helicopter is shown hovering over the British yacht, Camargue.

The unidentified crewman shown in this picture was saved during a rescue operation off South West England.

The Japanese were entering one such craft, the *Gekko Six*. Traditional crafts—such as America's *Tenacious*, England's *Morning Cloud*, and Bermuda's *Condor*—were veterans of competition, as were many of the sailors that manned them.

The race progressed smoothly with promise of a challenge. Some of the faster yachts had even navigated the Channel and were rounding Fastnet Rock when the winds increased. In a matter of hours, a challenging wind turned into gales of 75 miles per hour, hurricane force.

By Monday night, most of the sailors realized that this was an experience that would make Fastnet history.

Waves were said to have reached 40 feet, tossing crafts around like toy boats in a bathtub. The combined force of wind and sea held these yachts at their mercy. Boats were broken in half. Yachts were tossed in 360° flips. Even the most experienced crews were terrified. Yachts under 30 feet were more concerned with staying alive than they were with winning. SOS calls began to crackle over the ships' radios.

Many crews, after securing their ships, went below deck to wait out the storm. Others harnessed themselves to the main decks and were washed overboard when those harnesses broke. Masts broke in half and became dangerous obstacles to the other ships at sea. One sailor was thrown overboard with his ship's steering wheel grasped in his hands.

Finally, some ships were abandoned. Life boats split in two. Men clung to life in the rough seas, hoping that rescue would come.

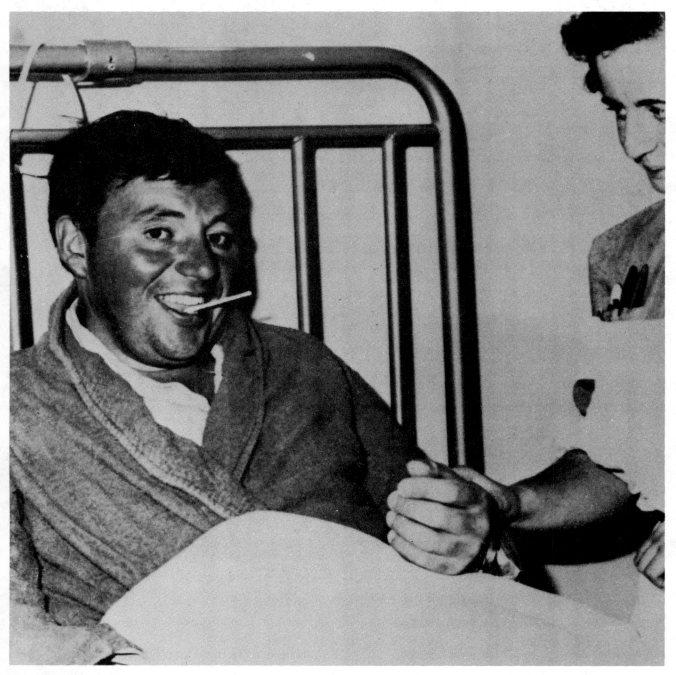

This crewman of the French yacht Tarantulla was rescued from his vessel by helicopter after he had abandoned ship.

The Irish yacht Regardless was towed into port with a snapped rudder. Gales devastated the new, lighter-weight crafts and smaller thirty-foot vessels.

Tuesday morning, the Royal Navy rescue station at Culdrose in Cornwall, England, was called to action. Due to vacation schedules, only two sea-rescue helicopters could be used. Civilian helicopters, jets, and a Dutch frigate soon followed to help.

The rescue crafts were hampered by wind, sea, and the yachts themselves. Waves bounced men back and forth like ping-pong balls, making the hovering rescue ropes difficult to reach. Some captains had to push their reluctant crews overboard in order to save them. One sailor who had jumped, died of exhaustion and exposure minutes prior to rescue.

The 35-foot American yacht, *Ariadne*, was spotted off the coast of Ireland, abandoned. One man, the *Ariadne's* captain, was pulled from the sea only to die later in a hospital.

No yacht was left unscathed. The crew of the *Kiola* reached port intact. The captain was rushed to the hospital with badly fractured ribs.

First place winner of the race was the American entry, *Tenacious*. But winning seemed of little importance against the loss of life and yachts. Of the 306 starting yachts, only 88 finished. At least 23 others were abandoned. One-hundred-and-thirty-six seamen were taken from the sea and 15 sailors died. Four people following the race in their own boat perished in the storm.

Could the loss of life and property have been avoided? Responsibility is hard to pinpoint, as no one can predict the sudden changes in nature.

The gale was particularly devastating to the new, lighter-weight crafts and the smaller 30-foot vessels. Should Fastnet officials prohibit these smaller boats from competing?

Should all entrants be required to have radio transmitters and receivers on board? Perhaps two-way communication would have aided and improved rescue attempts. Wherever the blame lie, the sea has proved that it is still a mistress to be courted gently.

FIRE AT THE MGM GRAND HOTEL

The fire which swept through the lower floors of the MGM Grand Hotel in Las Vegas began after dawn on November 21. Most of the guests in the 26-story hotel were asleep, although a few gamblers remained in the casino.

What wakened the sleeping guests, however, was not the fire but rather the billowing smoke and poisonous fumes which rose to the top of the hotel. Most of the 84 victims who died of smoke inhalation were trapped between the 19th and 24th floors.

The source of the fire was believed to be in the hotel's kitchen, and the time it began was shortly after 7 a.m. The flames quickly spread to the nearby casino, which was equipped with roulette wheels, craps tables, blackjack tables, slot machines — but no sprinkler system.

Billowing black smoke and noxious fumes poured out of the MGM Grand Hotel. The source of the fire, in which 84 lives were lost, was believed to be in the hotel's kitchen.

Hotel guests above the ninth floor could not be reached by firemen's ladders. Frightened guests leaned out of broken windows, hoping for rescue from the black smoke.

Behind the casino was the ''eye in the sky.'' This was a concealed catwalk fitted with one-way mirrors through which security guards could observe the gaming. Smoke and flames filled this catwalk and poured up elevator shafts and stairwells.

Although the fire never went above the second floor, it did damage the telephone switchboard as well as the fire alarm system. Those guests who were in their rooms had no warning of the fire, and an organized exodus became an impossibility. Panicked people made their way to exit doors only to find smoke-filled stairwells or worse, locked doors. Some were caught in hallways with no way to escape, while others died in their smoke-filled rooms.

Once the alarm had been sounded, dozens of fire trucks responded to the emergency. Fire ladders were used, but these only reached to the ninth floor of the hotel. Other firemen headed up the stairwells to lead guests from the higher floors to safety. Frightened guests were seen leaning from broken windows in an effort to escape the noxious black smoke.

Nearby Nellis Air Force Base rushed in helicopters to help those who had made their way to the roof. Cables were dropped from the helicopters, and hundreds of people were saved in this way. However, this operation had to be stopped as the draft created by the aircraft was fanning the fire.

Damage from the fire was estimated in the millions of dollars. However, money could not pay for the 84 lives which were lost or the 334 people who suffered injury.

The MGM Grand Hotel was built in 1973 and cost 106 million dollars. At the time it was built, it met the building code laws in effect. According to those laws, though, the only areas which required a sprinkler system were in the basement and on the first and top floors of the building. Although a new law was passed in 1979 requiring sprinklers on every floor and smoke detectors throughout the hotel, neither the sprinklers nor the smoke detectors were installed. Many lives which had been lost might have been saved if the new law had been complied with.

Later investigation into the fire showed that Clark County fire officials had found the MGM Grand lacking in adequate fire protection. The previous February, the hotel's owners had been requested to install more sprinklers as a condition for adding on to the hotel. These sprinklers were never installed.

Further investigation into the actual wreckage of the hotel showed gross violations of the fire laws. Gaping holes had even been cut into existing fire walls — walls which should have been solid — and, thus, allowed smoke to travel unchecked throughout the upper stories.

The MGM Grand Hotel had been the largest hotel in Las Vegas. After the fire, it was a shell of charred remains, broken glass and twisted steel. The saddest commentary on this fire which killed 84 people and injured over 300 more was that, with proper precautions, it might have been avoided.

Helicopters from Nellis Air Force Base were rushed in to help those who had made their way to the hotel's roof. Cables were dropped from the copters, and hundreds of people were saved in this way.

The killer earthquake which struck southern Italy left debris in its wake. Here, a lone man walks through what was once the town of Balvano.

It was Sunday night, and the villagers of southern Italy were doing what they usually did at the end of the day. Many were in their own homes, while others were attending evening Mass. In Balvano, some were receiving instructions for First Communion. Suddenly, at 7:36 p.m., the earth shook violently from Naples to Herculaneum — leaving death and destruction in its wake.

The part of southern Italy devastated by this earthquake extended over a 10,000-square-mile area. The cities of Naples and Salerno, the volcano Mt. Vesuvius, as well as the ancient cities of Pompeii and Herculaneum, all felt the shocks of this earthquake. The quake measured 6.8 on the Richter scale and was the strongest earthquake to hit Italy in the past 70 years.

The epicenter of the quake was at Eboli, about 30 miles southeast of Naples. The 32 aftershocks, though, were felt as far away as the island of Sicily in the south, to Trieste in the northeast and along the Yugoslav border.

The total area hit by the quake had been inhabited by approximately seven million people, many of whom lived in small villages on the sides of the mountains. Statistics show that over 2,900 persons died in the actual earthquake, many of them being buried alive under the rubble. Almost 8,000 more were injured as a result of the quake. However, the total number of dead may never be accurately compiled.

The farming town of Sant'Angelo dei Lombardi, located east of Naples, was a community of about 4,000 inhabitants. In a matter of seconds after the earthquake hit, all but a few buildings of the town lay in ruins. The official death toll here was several hundred, but about 1,000 persons were listed as missing.

In the hilltop town of Laviano, 1/3 of the residents were either missing or dead. The nearby village of Castelnuovo di Conza was completely destroyed—and the number of dead lying in the ruins unknown.

At The Church of Santa Maria Assunta in Balvano, some 300 parishoners—mostly mothers and children receiving instructions for First Communion—were attending evening Mass. Suddenly, the building was shaken to its foundation and the roof split in half. Many of those worshipping died under the stones of the church.

The remains of the small town of Avellino are shown here in this aerial view. Although the epicenter of the quake was at Eboli, 32 aftershocks were felt all over southern Italy.

Some victims dug out from underneath the debris by rescuers using their bare hands. The body shown here was carried by the firemen to a makeshift morgue.

To add to the magnitude of this disaster, the Italian authorities were not prepared. The first televised reports minimized the damage and the loss of life. In addition, bad roads and bad weather hampered the arrival of rescuers. In fact, some took more than two days to reach the afflicted areas. Soldiers, firemen and heavy equipment had to be sent from northern military bases hundreds of miles away. The lack of telephone communication further complicated relief efforts. Since the phone lines were

down, there was no way of getting information in or out of the damaged areas without going there in person.

Pope John Paul II and Italy's president, Allessandro Pertini, toured the stricken areas. However, their visits did not bring much comfort to those who desperately needed shovels for excavation, food for survival, and medicine to prevent the spread of disease.

In a disaster area where everything was needed, it is not surprising, although a bit horrifying, that a black

This scene of grieving relatives was a familiar one throughout southern Italy. Those who survived the quake had to face complete loss.

market trade flourished. The price of bottled water had doubled and the cost of a wooden coffin ran as high as $1,000. Those who lived to see the black market were bitter in their condemnation.

When the Italian government finally accepted the mammouth size of the disaster, outside help was sent in to the stricken areas. International aid came from the United States, Switzerland, West Germany and France — as well as from such far-off places as Japan and South Korea. Field hospitals were set up, and victims were treated as quickly as possible. Many of the survivors simply camped out in open spaces to avoid death from falling debris.

Destruction was so complete in some of the small villages that they had to be bulldozed and sprayed with disinfectant to prevent the spread of disease emanating from the rotting corpses.

The earthquake in southern Italy destroyed almost 100 towns and villages, killed over 2,900 people and injured 8,000 more. Bridges and roads were impassable and hundreds of thousands of people were left homeless. Before emergency housing could be adequately provided, the harshness of winter came to southern Italy. Thus, an already impoverished group of survivors had yet another obstacle with which to contend.

None who heard them will ever forget the cries of those who were buried alive under all the debris. Some of the victims were dug out by rescuers using their bare hands, only to die as they were freed. The horror of the earthquake which began on Sunday night at 7:36 p.m. will never be forgotten by any who survived the devastation wreaked by nature in 1980.

Bibliography

Briggs, Peter; *Rampage;* David McKay Company, Inc., New York; 1973

Brown, Walter R. and Anderson, Norman D.; *Fires;* Addison-Wesley Publishing Co., Reading, Mass.; 1976

Brown, Walter R. and Cutchen, Billye W.; *Floods;* Addison-Wesley Publishing Co., Reading, Mass.; 1975

Canning, John; *Great Disasters;* Longmeadow Press, Norwalk, Conn.; 1976

Drackett, Phil; *The Book of Great Disasters;* Purnell and Sons Limited, London; 1977

Facts on File; *Facts on File, Inc.,* New York, N.Y., 1979

Garrison, Webb; *Disasters that Made History;* Abingdon Press, Nashville and New York; 1973

Gelman, Woody and Jackson, Barbara; *Disaster Illustrated;* Harmony Books, New York, 1976

Haywood, Charles F.; *General Alarm;* Dodd, Mead & Company, New York; 1967

Hoehling, A. A.; *Disaster;* Hawthorn Books, Inc., New York; 1973

Jones, Michael Wynn; *Deadline Disaster;* David & Charles, Newton Abbot, London; 1976

Kennet, Frances; *Greatest Disasters of the 20th Century;* Castle Books, Secaucus, New Jersey; 1975

Lyons, Robert Paul; *Fire in America;* National Fire Protection Association, Boston, Mass.; 1976

Maloney, William E.; *The Great Disasters;* Grosset & Dunlap, New York; 1976

Menes, Aubrey; *London;* The Great Cities, Time-Life Book, Amsterdam; 1976

Nash, Jay Robert; *Darkest Hours;* Nelson Hall, Chicago; 1976

Rittmann, A. and L.; *Volcanoes;* G. P. Putnam's Sons, New York; 1976

Soule, Gardner; *Sea Rescue;* Macrae Smith Co., Philadelphia; 1966

Staff of Yankee, Inc.; *Danger, Disaster and Horrid Deeds;* Yankee, Inc., Dublin, New Hampshire; 1974

Wallechinsky, David and Wallace, Irving; *The People's Almanac #2;* Bantam Books, New York; 1978

Periodicals used include recent articles from the following:

Life Magazine
Newsweek
New York Times
Sports Illustrated
U.S. News & World Report

Photo Credits